CAMPAIGN • 250

THE MARETH LINE 1943

The end in Africa

KEN FORD

ILLUSTRATED BY STEVE NOON

Series editor Marcus Cowper

First published in Great Britain in 2012 by Osprey Publishing,
Midland House, West Way, Botley, Oxford OX2 0PH, UK
44-02 23rd St, Suite 219, Long Island City, NY 11101, USA

E-mail: info@ospreypublishing.com

ISBN: 978 1 78096 093 7
PDF e-book ISBN: 978 1 78096 094 4
E-pub e-book ISBN: 978 1 78096 095 1

Editorial by Ilios Publishing Ltd, Oxford, UK (www.iliospublishing.com)
Page layout by The Black Spot
Index by Auriol Griffith-Jones
Typeset in Myriad Pro and Sabon
Maps by Bounford.com
3D bird's-eye view by The Black Spot
Battlescene illustrations by Steve Noon
Originated by PDQ Media, Bungay, UK
Printed in China through Worldprint Ltd.

12 13 14 15 16   10 9 8 7 6 5 4 3 2 1

ARTIST'S NOTE

Readers may care to note that the original paintings from which the colour
plates in this book were prepared are available for private sale. The
Publishers retain all reproduction copyright whatsoever. All enquiries
should be addressed to:

Steve Noon, 50 Colchester Avenue, Penylan, Cardiff, CF23 9BP, UK

The Publishers regret that they can enter into no correspondence upon
this matter.

THE WOODLAND TRUST

Osprey Publishing is supporting the Woodland Trust, the UK's leading
woodland conservation charity, by funding the dedication of trees. To
celebrate the Queen's Diamond Jubilee we are proud to support the
Woodland Trust's Jubilee Woods Project.

IMPERIAL WAR MUSEUM COLLECTIONS

Many of the photos in this book come from the Imperial War Museum's
huge collections which cover all aspects of conflict involving Britain and
the Commonwealth since the start of the twentieth century.

These rich resources are available online to search, browse and buy at
www.iwmcollections.org.uk. In addition to Collections Online, you can
visit the Visitors Rooms where you can explore over 8 million photgraphs,
thousands of hours of moving images, the largest sound archive of its
kind in the world, thousands of diaries and letters written by people
in wartime, and a huge reference library. To make an appointment call
(020) 7416 5320, or email mail@iwm.org.uk. Imperial War Museum
www.iwm.org.uk.

Key to military symbols

XXXXX	XXXX	XXX	XX	X	III	II
Army Group	Army	Corps	Division	Brigade	Regiment	Battalion
I	•••	••	•	Infantry	Artillery	Cavalry
Company/Battery	Platoon	Section	Squad			
Airborne	Unit HQ	Air defence	Air Force	Air mobile	Air transportable	Amphibious
Anti-tank	Armour	Air aviation	Bridging	Engineer	Headquarters	Maintenance
Medical	Missile	Mountain	Navy	Nuclear, biological, chemical	Ordnance	Parachute
Reconnaissance	Signal	Supply	Transport movement	Rocket artillery	Air defence artillery	

Key to unit identification

Unit identifier — Parent unit

Commander

(+) with added elements
(–) less elements

ORIGINS OF THE BATTLE

On 4 November 1942, the defeat of Panzerarmee Afrika under the command of Generalfeldmarschall (GFM) Erwin Rommel by Lieutenant-General (Lt. Gen.) Bernard Montgomery's Eighth Army in the battle of El Alamein proved to be the climax of the Desert War. The struggle that had begun in September 1940 against Italian forces on the Libyan–Egyptian border had by then reached its critical moment – a trial of strength in which a dramatic breakthrough would have been possible by whoever proved to be the most determined. It was Montgomery who succeeded.

The conflict in North Africa had progressed from a fight between two colonial powers into a theatre of war which captured the attention of the whole world. After Britain's repulse in the Battle of France in June 1940 and its exit from the continent of Europe through Dunkirk, the North African desert was the only place in which its land forces opposed the enemy.

The theatre was the scene of many large-scale battles, especially after Italian troops were joined by those from their ally Germany under the command of Erwin Rommel. Actions were fought over wide-open tracts of desert in a harsh environment that punished the unwary. As one side moved away from its supply bases, the other side grew closer to its own. Growing strength on one side was met with gradual weakening on the other. Progress

A soldier examines an Italian M13/14 tank that had been knocked out at Alamein. (DA-02734, War History Collection, Alexander Turnbull Library, Wellington NZ)

LEFT
Italian prisoners in captivity after the battle. Most had been left behind without transport as the Germans rushed away from the battlefield in their tanks and trucks. (IWM, E21541)

RIGHT
A New Zealand padre conducts a burial service for some of the fallen at El Alamein. (DA-11753, War History Collection, Alexander Turnbull Library, Wellington NZ)

was a to-and-fro trek between the deserts of Libya and Egypt as each side in turn gained the upper hand.

Over a period of more than two years, many leading commanders had seen their reputations won or lost in the desert through the battles they had fought. The disaster of the loss of Tenth Army by the Italian commander Graziani was in great contrast to the success gained by Lieutenant-General Richard O'Connor, whose outflanking movements across vast wastes were later employed by Rommel. This initial success was soon followed by General Archibald Wavell's efforts throughout 1941. With few resources and the need to supply troops to diversions in Greece and Crete, Wavell's command brought little reward. Auchinleck, who followed him, could count the successes of Operation *Crusader* and First Alamein amongst his battle honours, but he, like Wavell, fell victim to Prime Minister Winston Churchill's impatience for greater victories.

The Desert War was dominated by the charismatic German commander Erwin Rommel. After his arrival in Libya on 12 February 1941, the situation changed completely. Rommel brought with him the units that were to become the famed Deutsches Afrika Korps (DAK). His expertise, daring exploits and bold leadership created a type of warfare that had the British reacting to his moves. There is little doubt that his superiority in generalship, and the greater effectiveness of his tanks and weapons, always placed his opponents at a disadvantage. His greatest problem was one of supply and it was this shortcoming that compromised his plan to capture Egypt and cross the Suez Canal into the Middle East. Whether this might actually have been a possibility remains a subject for historians to debate, but there is little doubt that if his Panzerarmee Afrika had had sufficient strength to go on the offensive at Alamein, the outcome of the Desert War might have been quite different.

Lieutenant-General Bernard Montgomery had arrived in Egypt at a most opportune moment. General Claude Auchinleck before him had by then halted Rommel's advance into Egypt and had won the first battle of El Alamein. When Montgomery took over Eighth Army in August 1942, he had only part of Auchinleck's old command to deal with. Auchinleck before him was Commander-in-Chief Middle East and had responsibility for the war in North Africa and for the troubles in Iraq, Persia, Palestine, etc. Montgomery was given just Eighth Army and reported to General Sir Harold Alexander who held responsibility for the remainder of the Middle East. Montgomery also

Field guns of the Italian Divisione Corrazzata 'Ariete' left on the battlefield after Alamein. The division suffered appalling losses and very few men or tanks survived to begin the retreat. (DA-11211, War History Collection, Alexander Turnbull Library, Wellington NZ)

had the luxury of not attacking until Eighth Army had been massively reinforced, retrained and had plentiful supplies. This superiority in numbers of troops, weapons and new skills after so many years of having to make do with what was available, was the means with which he was able to overwhelm Rommel on the battlefield.

The British Eighth Army that Rommel and his Panzerarmee Afrika faced at El Alamein was, at that time, the most powerful formation that Britain had put into the war. If it had been defeated then the whole of the nation's presence in the Middle East would have been compromised. Both sides had fought at El Alamein knowing that failure would mean the end. For his part Rommel understood that if he could not overwhelm Eighth Army, then he could not stay in Egypt or possibly even remain in Libya. Montgomery also knew of the importance of winning. He realized that if he failed, it would be months, or even years, before Eighth Army could regain Egypt and rebuild its strength to go on the offensive again.

A South African-built Marmon Herrington armoured car passes a burning Panzer after the battle of Alamein. The picture appears to have been set up for the cameraman, for the tank looks as though it had been wrecked some time earlier and a small fire started on it for effect. (IWM, E23088)

The eventual success by the British at El Alamein ensured that they would remain masters of North Africa, provided that the Axis forces were not given the opportunity to re-form and strike back. On paper, on 4 November, the probability of the enemy striking back seemed very unlikely. The victory had been so complete that the Italian–German army could do little but flee. Its annihilation at the hands of the massed British armour that was gathering ready to pursue it looked inevitable. History, however, shows that in the months following Alamein, Rommel and his men did escape, they did re-form and they did attempt to strike back. Eighth Army proved unable to administer the final blow on its own. Rommel escaped into Tunisia with his Axis forces and it took the combined strength of two Allied armies finally to chase them from Africa.

This second Allied army was the result of an Anglo-American invasion of North Africa on 8 November 1942. Operation *Torch*, commanded by General Dwight D. Eisenhower, brought a new force into the theatre when Americans arrived to fight the Axis forces. They quickly moved into Tunisia and stationed themselves in Rommel's rear. Hitler reacted to this Allied move by immediately ordering Tunis to be seized by the few German troops already in the country and for new forces, under the command of Generaloberst Hans-Jürgen von Arnim, to be airlifted over the Mediterranean to defend the city. The speed of this deployment over the next days and weeks was formidable and took the Allies by surprise. Within 14 days there were enough Germans in Tunisia to stifle the Allied move on Tunis and to keep the city and most of Tunisia under Nazi control for six more months.

CHRONOLOGY

1942

4 November   The battle of El Alamein reaches its conclusion with a victory for Lt. Gen. Montgomery's Eighth Army and a defeat for GFM Rommel's Panzerarmee Afrika.

5 November   Rommel's forces are in full retreat and Montgomery's armoured formations give chase, trying to cut off and capture as many of the enemy as possible by various manoeuvres across the desert.

6 November   Attempts to trap the fleeing Axis forces at Fuka fail.

8 November   Operation *Torch* lands Anglo-American forces in North Africa. These forces are gradually enlarged to form First Army. Rommel now has an enemy army to his front and his rear.

11 November   After managing to evade being captured at Mersa Matruh, Rommel and his army cross over the Sollum Heights into Libya.

13 November   Eighth Army reaches Tobruk and finds that Rommel's forces have gone.

19 November   Axis forces pull out of Benghazi and retreat into the El Agheila positions.

14 December   Montgomery launches his attack at El Agheila but finds that the bulk of Rommel's army has pulled out, falling back on a new line at Buerat.

1943

14 January   Anticipating Eighth Army's attack, Panzerarmee Afrika withdraws from Buerat towards a new position at Homs.

15 January   Montgomery attacks the Buerat Line only to find that most of the enemy have departed leaving just rearguards behind.

20 January   Rommel has no intention of holding the line at Homs or the port of Tripoli, and starts a staged withdrawal which will take him from Libya into Tunisia and the defences of the Mareth Line.

23 January   Eighth Army arrives in Tripoli to much celebration.

15 February   Eighth Army begins arriving in force in the area in front of the Mareth Line. Its long supply chain stretching back hundreds of kilometres is severely stretched and it will take weeks before it is ready to mount an assault.

17 February   Rommel uses the pause to exploit the exposed nature of the Anglo-American force in Tunisia and helps Gen. von Arnim's 5. Panzerarmee to launch a surprise attack on the Americans at Kasserine.

6 March   Generale Messe, now in command of what has become Italian First Army, launches, at Rommel's suggestion, a spoiling attack on Montgomery's forces before they are ready to launch their own attack on the Mareth defences. Operation *Capri* fails miserably.

9 March GFM Rommel leaves Africa never to return.

20 March Montgomery launches Operation *Pugilist* against the Mareth Line. Its limited strength of just one division, 50th Division, is not capable of withstanding a counterattack by 15. Panzer-Division and is forced back to its start line. An outflanking move by New Zealand Corps through the Tebaga Gap also fails.

23 March Montgomery changes his plans and decides to make the Tebaga Gap his main assault and reinforces the New Zealand Corps with HQ X Corps and 1st Armoured Division.

26 March Lt. Gen. Horrocks' X Corps launches Operation *Supercharge II* and drives through the Tebaga Gap to outflank the defences at Mareth. The enemy retreats north of Gabes to a new position at Wadi Akarit.

6 April Eighth Army attacks the enemy line at Wadi Akarit. By the end of the day, after heavy fighting, Gen. Messe realizes that the position is untenable and gives the order for a retreat to a new position at Enfidaville 240km to the north.

16 April Eighth Army closes up to positions at Enfidaville but intends to execute only limited attacks leaving First Army to continue the drive towards Tunis.

3 May First Army launches Operation *Strike*, the final offensive to take Tunis.

13 May All Axis forces in Tunisia surrender to the Allies; the war in North Africa is over.

OPPOSING COMMANDERS

Many of the commanders from both sides who fought at El Alamein had been in the theatre for a long time. Some, like Montgomery, had been relatively new arrivals who had brought new ideas to a desert war that had been dragging on for more than two years. Each of them, however, had to acclimatize to an inhospitable battlefield like no other. The wide-open spaces allowed great boldness of action, provided forces were mobile enough and well led, but the empty barren landscape was also quick to punish those commanders who did not pay due regard to their administration arm. More than in any other theatre of war, it was the supply train that dictated the tactics that could be employed on the battlefield. This was especially true during the long retreat of Rommel's army and the great pursuit undertaken by Montgomery.

BRITISH COMMANDERS

Although Gen. Montgomery was the architect of the victory of El Alamein, he was not the most senior commander in the region. He reported to the Commander-in-Chief Middle East, **Gen. Sir Harold Alexander (1891–1969)**, an aristocratic guardsman of great charm and ability who was responsible for military events, not only in North Africa, but also in the whole of Palestine, Iraq and Persia. He had served as a divisional commander with some distinction during the campaign in France in 1940 and in Burma after the Japanese invasion. A great favourite of Churchill, he had many friends in high places and was for a time ADC to the King. He was also, in October 1937, the youngest general in the British Army.

Alexander's main attribute was one of diplomacy. He had the ability to organize and persuade, without having to resort to threats and dictates. Although responsible for the strategy of the North African campaign, he was more than happy to leave this matter and general tactical considerations to his subordinate Montgomery. His talents were later put to good use when the USA joined in the conflict in North Africa, for Alexander's capacity for getting along with people proved to be a great asset when he became the army group commander of 18th Army Group, responsible for both the Anglo-American First Army and Montgomery's Eighth Army during the Tunisian campaign.

General Bernard Montgomery (1887–1976) made his lasting reputation through the victory at El Alamein. Before that time he was virtually unknown to the British public. He was, however, very well known within army circles.

He had built a reputation as an outspoken critic of various military practices and of indifferent and incompetent commanders. His experiences in France in 1940 as a divisional and corps commander led him to think that there was much wrong in the British Army and he never lost an opportunity to explain how things should be put right. He had great conviction in his own ability and always believed that his approach to battle was the only way. In his operations he was often seen as an overcautious commander, only going into the attack when everything was in his favour and he was virtually assured of success.

Montgomery was fortunate that his arrival at Eighth Army in August 1942 coincided with the influx into Egypt of great quantities of new supplies, arms, equipment and reinforcements, things that had been denied to previous commanders. He also was given – or in fact took – sufficient time to retrain his army to his way of thinking before he was prepared to launch his Alamein offensive. There is no doubt that he transformed Eighth Army for the better in every department, not least by being ruthless with those commanders who did not come up to his expectations. On a more personal note, his prickly character and insufferable arrogance often seemed offensive to some, leaving many detractors in his wake, but his fighting men idolized him. They appreciated his raising of Eighth Army's profile in the world and they loved him for it. After Alamein they knew they were part of a successful army and, as it turned out, one that was never beaten in battle again.

Montgomery always wanted to select his own commanders, those who were already in position wherever he arrived were usually moved on. After Alamein, Montgomery looked closely at the performance of some of his senior commanders and decided few changes had to be made. Two of his corps commanders, Lt. Gen. Leese and Lt. Gen. Horrocks, both individuals that he had brought to the theatre, had proved their worth at Alamein and remained to fight under Montgomery in other campaigns. Lieutenant-General Herbert Lumsden was not so blessed, for he and his divisional commanders were often at odds with Montgomery over armoured tactics.

Lieutenant-General Oliver Leese (1894–1978) and **Lt. Gen. Brian Horrocks (1895–1985)** had both served in France at the same time as Montgomery in 1940, Leese at Lord Gort's HQ and Horrocks as a battalion commander in

Monty's division. Their subsequent performance in England led him to think that they were capable of corps command. **Lieutenant-General Herbert Lumsden (1897–1945)** was a cavalry officer who was already in Egypt when Montgomery arrived. He had a good deal of experience in armoured warfare, first at the head of 1st Armoured Division, then as commander of X Corps which contained the three British armoured divisions. Monty was not happy with Lumsden's handling of the tanks throughout Alamein and became less convinced that he could lead the corps during the initial pursuit after the battle. Horrocks replaced him at the head of X Corps in December 1942.

After the *Torch* invasion of North Africa by an Anglo-American force led by **Gen. Dwight D. Eisenhower (1890–1969)** the whole command structure changed. What was purely a British and Commonwealth battleground then became an Allied one. Eisenhower was eventually to take over the whole of the theatre as Commander-in-Chief Allied Force Headquarters [North Africa]. A new army, First Army, commanded by **Lt. Gen. Kenneth Anderson (1891–1959)**, came into being in Tunisia in late 1942. When Eighth Army finally reached Tunisia early in 1943, First and Eighth Armies were combined into 18th Army Group under the command of Alexander, with Eisenhower being responsible for the whole North African campaign. From this point on, Montgomery was no longer master of the battlefield; he now had to share the making of decisions which affected overall Allied strategy with others.

AXIS COMMANDERS

The long Axis chain of command in North Africa was made particularly complex by the Italian nature of the theatre. Libya was an Italian colony and all the fighting that took place in North Africa up to and beyond Alamein was officially under Italian direction. Mussolini had asked Hitler for German help back in 1941 and had always considered that his commanders were in control of the strategy and the tactics to be used in the campaign. The reality was, however, that once Erwin Rommel arrived he took over the running of the show. In theory, Rommel reported to the Governor of Libya, Maresciallo Ettore Bastico, who in turn reported to the Commando Supremo in Rome, Maresciallo Ugo Cavallero. When Rommel's army had retreated into Tunisia, command at the top changed. As Panzerarmee Afrika was now out of Libya, Bastico ceased to have a territory to command and was removed from the scene. Also at about this time, Cavallero stepped aside and was replaced by

Generalfeldmarschall Erwin Rommel, the Desert Fox. As the campaign in North Africa neared its climax, Rommel's health had deteriorated to such an extent that he was recalled to Germany for rest. By then, Hitler and Mussolini had lost patience with his continual pleading for withdrawals and more withdrawals and believed he had lost the will to stand and fight. (battlefieldhistorian.com)

the World War I veteran **Maresciallo Vittorio Ambrosio (1979–1958)** as Commando Supremo. To complicate matters further for Rommel, his immediate German superior was the Luftwaffe Generalfeldmarschall Albert Kesselring, C.-in-C. German Forces Mediterranean. Thus Rommel had three immediate masters to please, although in practice he seldom took the trouble to please any of them.

Generalfeldmarschall Erwin Rommel (1891–1944) had enhanced his already formidable reputation before he arrived in North Africa. One of Hitler's favourite generals, he had seen impressive service as an armoured commander in the campaign in Poland in 1939 and France in 1940. His numerous victories against the British in Libya and Egypt and his bold use of mobile forces marked him out to be something special. His victory at Gazala in May 1942, together with the capture of Tobruk and the advance into Egypt, threatened the whole of Britain's Middle East strategy. He appeared to be invincible and was certainly admired by friend and foe alike. In the end the vast nature of the desert battlefields and the problems of keeping his army supplied led to his defeat at Alamein.

At the time of Alamein, Rommel's command was Panzerarmee Afrika. In Tunisia this formation was renamed German–Italian Panzerarmee (Deutsch-Italienische Panzerarmee) and then finally First Italian Army and given the more familiar abbreviation AOK 1.

Generalleutnant Wilhelm Ritter von Thoma, commander of the Afrika Korps, was captured by the British at the end of the Alamein battle and his place at the head of the German armoured formation was taken by **General der Panzertruppen Gustav Fehn (1892–1945)**, an infantry officer who switched to armour at the beginning of the war. Fehn commanded 5. Panzer-Division and then XXXX Panzer-Korps before moving to Africa in November 1942. The last commander of the Afrika Korps was **General der Panzertruppen Hans Cramer (1896–1968)** who took over after Fehn was wounded in January 1943. Cramer had arrived in the theatre with 15. Panzer-Division's Panzer-Regiment 8 in April 1941, but was severely wounded during the British *Battleaxe* offensive in June.

Most of the troops in Panzerarmee Afrika were Italian. The performance of their commanders varied. Some had Rommel's support, whilst others left him in a state of despair. **Generale di Corpo d'Armata Giuseppe de Stephanis (1885–1965)** was one of the better leaders. He had commanded the Divisione Corrazzata 'Ariete' before taking over the Italian XX Corpo for the battle at Alamein. Of all the Italian commanders, Rommel regarded **Generale di Corpo d'Armata Enea Navarini** as his 'trusted friend'. Navarini commanded the Italian XXI Corpo through the long retreat into the Mareth Line.

To counter the Allied landings in North Africa and their invasion of Tunisia, the Germans raised a new army under the command of **Generaloberst Hans-Jürgen von Arnim (1899–1962)**. This new formation, 5. Panzerarmee Afrika, (later to be shortened to PzAOK 5), controlled most of eastern and central Tunisia. Arnim had previously commanded 17. Panzer-Division and XXXIC Korps on the Eastern Front. When Rommel brought his Panzerarmee Afrika into the defences around Mareth, thought could then be given to combining these two formations into an army group command. Rommel by this time was seen as being overtired and ill and was to be returned to Germany for rest, so Arnim was given command of the new Heeresgruppe Afrika (Army Group Africa), but only after Rommel had left the theatre. Rommel's position at the head of the German–Italian

Army was then taken over by the Italian **Maresciallo Giovanni Messe (1883–1968)**. Messe was a veteran of the Great War and later saw a good deal of service with the Italians in their early campaigns in Ethiopia, Albania and Greece. In Russia he commanded Corpo di Spedizione Italiano. When the Italian Commando Supremo decided that Rommel had to be replaced, Messe seemed to be the obvious candidate with the most battle experience.

With Messe in overall command, the famed Afrika Korps now had to report to an Italian master. **Oberst Fritz Bayerlein (1899–1970)** was Rommel's Chief of Staff and when he left the theatre Bayerlein acted more or less in the same capacity, as German liaison officer to Messe. As one-time temporary commander of the Afrika Korps, he took great pains to look after that formation's best interests and often ignored orders from the Italians if they went against his natural instincts. Bayerlein developed hepatitis in Tunisia and was invalided back to Germany and hence escaped capture when the Axis forces there collapsed in May 1943. He later commanded the 3. Panzer-Division in Russia and the Panzer 'Lehr' Division in Normandy and the Rhineland. Just before the end of the war he was given a corps command on the western front.

OPPOSING ARMIES

The contrast between the British and Axis forces at the end of the battle at El Alamein could not have been greater. British Eighth Army had ground out a great victory and was poised to exploit this triumph by annihilating its enemy. Panzerarmee Afrika was defeated, scattered and broken to the extent that, for a while, command and control had almost ceased to exist.

BRITISH FORCES

As a result of the difficulties in shipping supplies across the Mediterranean Sea, Axis forces were always short of weapons and ammunition. In contrast, Eighth Army's supply situation was much more satisfactory. Allied convoys to the great supply dumps in Egypt were routed around South Africa and up to the southern end of the Suez Canal along much safer sea routes. Great quantities of new *matériel* were thus constantly available to Montgomery's army, including many of the latest weapons. By the start of the fourth year of the war in late 1942, new developments in weapons technology were reaching the battlefield from the production line.

One of the best new weapons was the 17-pdr anti-tank gun which arrived in Egypt in December and proved to be a very potent weapon against German

Motorcycle dispatch riders in the desert. With all radio traffic liable to be intercepted by the other side, the only safe way of transmitting orders and information was by human hand. The task of locating isolated units, camouflaged from spying eyes and dispersed across a flat featureless landscape, was a difficult one for these motorcyclists. (DA-00265, War History Collection, Alexander Turnbull Library, Wellington NZ)

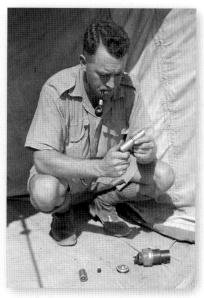

tanks. Virtually all of the 2-pdr anti-tank guns had by then been replaced by great numbers of the excellent 6-pdr. The 6-pdr gun had also been used to up-gun Crusader and Valentine tanks, but the move was not very successful; the Crusader still remained unreliable and the Valentine lost its hull machine gun in the process. However, the arrival of quantities of American Sherman tanks more than made up for the poor-performing British models. Their 75mm M3 guns were a great improvement on the main armament of the Grant. Also arriving in numbers was the Churchill Mark III tank with a 6-pdr gun. This heavy infantry tank was mechanically reliable with good armoured protection.

A feature of Eighth Army was the effectiveness of its artillery. There were ample supplies of both 25-pdr field guns and 5.5in. medium artillery pieces. Every attack launched by Montgomery's forces was supported by a great weight of artillery fire. Later in the campaign the arrival of the 7.2in. howitzer provided impressive support in the attack. Its greater range (15,600m) and heavier shell gave good service against the fixed defences of the Mareth Line.

After Alamein some changes were made in the composition of Eighth Army with several formations disappearing from the theatre. The 8th Armoured Division had never seen action as a division and was disbanded two months after Alamein. The 10th Armoured Division began the pursuit, but was withdrawn after just three days and returned to Egypt for a refit, but never fought as a complete armoured formation again. The 44th Infantry Division was also broken up and dispersed after the battle. The Australian 9th Division was shipped back to Australia after Alamein to help bolster the nation's defences when Japan had entered the war. The South African 1st Division returned to its homeland in December to be reconstituted as an armoured division. There was one addition to Eighth Army's formations in Tunisia after the Mareth Line battle when 56th Infantry Division arrived to join Montgomery's forces.

With Eighth Army during the pursuit was a contingent of Free French forces under the command of Gen. Philippe Leclerc (a *nom de guerre* adopted to protect his family in France). The group was nominally given the name 'L' Force and consisted of 555 French and 2,713 Colonial and African troops. The party had fought its way across the desert from the Chad region of

LEFT
A Bofors 40mm anti-aircraft gun keeps watch for Luftwaffe fighters as a well-dispersed convoy of trucks in the background makes its way across the desert. (IWM, E21873)

RIGHT
A New Zealand soldier examines an Italian anti-personnel 'thermos bomb'. This weapon was dropped from aircraft and detonated if it was picked up or moved. Its name derived from its appearance which was similar to a common thermos drinking flask. The first New Zealander 'killed in action' casualty was a victim of this device in September 1940. (DA-00634, War History Collection, Alexander Turnbull Library, Wellington NZ)

French Equatorial Africa to meet up with Montgomery's forces at Tripoli. It comprised camel and horse cavalry, some motorized infantry and a few guns. Also with Eighth Army from the days before Alamein was the Free French Flying Column, a small unit which consisted of two armoured car squadrons, one tank company (11 Crusaders and two Shermans) and two lorried platoons of infantry.

Protecting the skies above Eighth Army and giving support to actions on the ground was the Desert Air Force. The formation was building a steady reputation for itself through its organization and tactical ability. It had two major roles: first, to deny airspace to the enemy and, second, to support ground troops. The arrival of more Spitfire squadrons allowed it to deal with any appearance by the Luftwaffe. The concept of tactical air support was refined by the use of fighter-bombers working under the direction of forward air controllers located at the front with the leading army units. Tank-busting Hurricane fighters firing two 40mm cannons added to its armoury.

AXIS FORCES

The roll-call of Rommel's forces at the end of Alamein made depressing reading for Panzerarmee Afrika. It had entered the battle with a strong balance of infantry and armour, but much of this was decimated during the battle. It was true that the bulk of the infantry was Italian and was from divisions with little mobility suitable only for defence and consolidation, but the armour contained two crack armoured divisions within the Afrika Korps along with fairly competent, although less effective, Italian tank formations. In total Rommel had, under his command, three Italian corps containing, four infantry divisions, one parachute division, one motorized division and two armoured divisions. His German troops consisted of one armoured corps, two armoured divisions and two light divisions. Alamein changed all that.

On the morning of 4 November, the day on which the battle was deemed to have ended, the British Official History summed up the state of the Axis forces: 'The enemy's losses were tremendous, the German formations being reduced to skeletons and the Italian broken to bits.' It stated that the Italian armoured divisions 'Trento', 'Trieste' and motorized division 'Littorio' had been almost wiped out. All other German and Italian formations had been 'severely mauled'. Rommel had no clear picture of these losses in the chaos that followed the collapse. All he knew was that he had just 38 German tanks left out of a total of 249 that started the action.

The next day the Afrika Korps reported rough estimates of its strength; 15. Panzer-Division had eight tanks, 200 infantry, four anti-tank guns and 12 field guns left. None of its 88mm guns had survived. Much the same losses were also true for 21. Panzer-Division; it had 30 tanks, 400 infantry, 16 anti-tank guns, 25 field guns and no 88mm guns. The 164. leichte-Division had just 600 officers and men from its three *Panzergrenadier* regiments intact after the battle, again without any 88mm guns.

As for prisoners, 2,922 Germans and 4,148 Italians had been captured during the battle. More were to follow into captivity over the next few days as many of those fleeing the battlefield were rounded up. Most of the Italians were trying to make their escape on foot. Six days later the numbers had risen to 7,802 Germans and 22,071 Italians, almost 30,000 men in total.

It was from this sorry state of affairs that Rommel attempted to rebuild his army and evade total destruction. The poor supply situation forced the Axis army to work hard at salvaging and repairing weapons to keep them in service. What new weapons there were reached North Africa only spasmodically.

LEFT
A German PzKpfw III Special with the longer 50mm gun lies abandoned on the desert floor. It looks undamaged and may well have just run out of fuel when trying to escape. (IWM, E21851)

RIGHT
A heavy German field gun and its half-tracked tractor which had been knocked out by New Zealand artillery near Gabes. (DA-06910, War History Collection, Alexander Turnbull Library, Wellington NZ)

LEFT
German troops manning a defensive line in the desert, armed with an 80mm mortar. (DA-08295, War History Collection, Alexander Turnbull Library, Wellington NZ)

RIGHT
Italian troops in their own transport arrive into British lines to surrender after the capitulation of Axis forces in Tunisia. (DA-02049, War History Collection, Alexander Turnbull Library, Wellington NZ)

BOTTOM
Men of the New Zealand Division's light cavalry relax on the top of their Stuart tank in a quiet moment between the action. (DA-02569, War History Collection, Alexander Turnbull Library, Wellington NZ)

The new 75mm Pak 40 anti-tank gun began arriving once Panzerarmee Afrika had reached Tunisia, as did the redesigned 88mm Flak 41 gun which had been modified for anti-tank use with a lower silhouette and an improved shield. Its formidable hitting power remained undiminished.

During the first days of the retreat, more and more individuals who had evaded capture by trekking across barren terrain avoiding squadrons of tanks and roaming armoured cars rejoined their formations. One notable group of these stragglers turned up at Rommel's battlewagon headquarters on 7 November. Generalmajor Ramcke had brought with him 600 survivors from his Parachute brigade, along with some men of the Italian Divisione 'Folgore', who had all been abandoned on the southern sector of the Alamein defences whilst the rest of their comrades fled. They trekked north-west across barren desert to join the remainder of the Axis army, fighting their way out of the trap laid by British armoured cars and reconnaissance troops.

As Rommel's retreat continued and he attempted to make various defensive stands and rearguard actions, losses continued to mount. However, some reinforcements began to arrive over rapidly shortening supply lines to offset these losses. Some battered formations were amalgamated or disbanded while others who were newly arrived in the theatre, mostly Italian, were sent forwards as an advance guard. Newly arrived during the retreat were the 80^a Divisione 'La Spezia' and 16^a Divisione Motorizzate 'Pistoia'. The net result was a gathering strength, although never strong enough to commit to a full pitched battle or even a long and resolute defence of any given position. It was strong enough to keep Montgomery's forces at arm's length, but not strong enough to stop them.

ORDERS OF BATTLE

BRITISH ORDER OF BATTLE AT MARETH

Allied 18th Army Group Gen. Sir Harold Alexander
Eighth Army Gen. Sir Bernard Montgomery
New Zealand Corps Lt. Gen. Sir Bernard C. Freyberg
2nd New Zealand Division Lt. Gen. Sir Bernard C. Freyberg
    NZ 5th Infantry Brigade
    NZ 6th Infantry Brigade
8th Independent Armoured Brigade Brig. Edward Custance
French 'L' Force Général de Division Philippe Leclerc

XXX Corps Lt. Gen. Oliver Leese
50th (Northumbrian) Division Maj. Gen. J. S. Nichols
    69th Infantry Brigade
    150th Infantry Brigade
    151st Infantry Brigade

51st (Highland) Division Maj. Gen. D. N. Wimberley
    152nd Infantry Brigade
    153rd Infantry Brigade
    154th Infantry Brigade

4th Indian Division Maj. Gen. F. I. S. Tuker
    5th Indian Brigade
    7th Indian Brigade
    11th Indian Brigade

201st Guards Motor Brigade Brig. J. Gascoigne

X Corps Lt. Gen. Brian Horrocks
1st Armoured Division Maj. Gen. R. Briggs
    2nd Armoured Brigade
    7th Motor Brigade

7th Armoured Division Maj. Gen. G. Erskine
    4th Light Armoured Brigade
    22nd Armoured Brigade
    131st Brigade

AXIS ORDER OF BATTLE AT MARETH
Heeresgruppe Afrika (Army Group Africa)
Generaloberst Hans-Jürgen von Arnim
First Italian Army Generale di Corpo Giovanni Messe
Italian XX Corpo Generale di Divisione Taddeo Orlando

136^a Divisione Giovani Fascisti Generale di Divisione Nino Sozzani
    136° Reggimento di Fanteria Giovani Fascisti
    8° Reggimento Bersaglieri

101^a Divisione 'Trieste' Generale di Brigata Francesco La Ferla
    65° Reggimento Valtellini
    66° Reggimento Valtellini

90. leichte-Afrika-Division Generalmajor Theodor Graf von Sponeck
    Infanterie-Regiment 155
    Infanterie-Regiment 200
    Infanterie-Regiment 361
    Panzer-Regiment Afrika

Italian XXI Corpo Generale di Corpo d'Armata Paolo Berardi
80^a Divisione 'La Spezia' Generale di Brigata Gavino Pizzolato
    125° Reggimento di Fanteria
    126° Reggimento di Fanteria

16^a Divisione Motorizzate 'Pistoia' Generale di Brigata Giuseppe Falugi
    35° Pistoia Reggimento Pistoia
    36° Pistoia Reggimento Pistoia

German 164. leichte-Afrika-Division Generalmajor Kurt Freiherr von Liebenstein
    Panzergrenadier-Regiment 125
    Panzergrenadier-Regiment 382
    Panzergrenadier-Regiment 433

19. Flak Division (Luftwaffe) Generalmajor Gothard Frantz

Raggruppamento Sahariano (Saharan Group) Generale di Brigata Alberto Mannerini

Deutsches Afrika Korps (DAK) General der Panzertruppen Hans Cramer
15. Panzer-Division Generalleutnant Willibald Borowietz
    Panzer-Regiment 8
    Panzergrenadier-Regiment 115

21. Panzer-Division Generalmajor Heinrich-Hermann von Hülsen
    Panzer-Regiment 5
    Panzergrenadier-Regiment 104

In reserve with PzAOK 5, but subject to call.

10. Panzer-Division Generalleutnant Friedrich Freiherr von Broich
    Panzer-Regiment 7
    Panzergrenadier-Regiment 69

OPPOSING PLANS

The scale of the defeat suffered by Rommel at El Alamein in November 1942 sealed the fate of Panzerarmee Afrika at a time when the progress of the war was turning inexorably against the Axis powers: Hitler's attack on Russia was going badly, with the crisis at Stalingrad nearing its peak; Eighth Army was daily growing in strength as new supplies and reinforcements were arriving in Egypt and the entry of the USA into the war the previous year now meant that its great industrial powerhouse was being added to the Allied cause. Three of the four major world powers were united against Germany and Italy, all readying themselves to grind down the fascist dictatorships.

It did not take long for Rommel to understand that his campaign in North Africa was a hopeless cause. Over the last year it had been proving more and more difficult to ferry the great quantities of supplies and arms that he needed across the Mediterranean Sea. Fuel was his greatest worry, for he never seemed to have enough to engage in the type of mobile warfare for which he was famous. After Alamein, he was constantly plagued by shortages. Again and again his tanks and transport remained idle in the desert during the retreat, waiting for fuel to be lorried forwards along supply lines hundreds of kilometres long. This lack of petrol was also mirrored by the lack of almost every other item that an army finds essential whilst on campaign, from tanks and troops to water and food. All were in constant short supply.

The weakest link in the supply chain was the route across the Mediterranean Sea. Virtually every convoy and every individual ship that tried to make the short trip was attacked by the Royal Navy or the RAF either at sea or when tied up in port. A great advantage for the British was their ability to break German codes. Intercepted signals allowed Royal Navy submarines to be tipped off about sailings from Italian ports and intercept them. Any ships that managed to run the gauntlet of open water and make it to a friendly harbour, faced attacks by RAF bombers.

The code breakers also informed the Royal Navy when the Italian Navy planned to send out its capital ships to protect a convoy. British battleships and aircraft carriers based in Gibraltar and Alexandria then put to sea and attempted to bring them to battle. Of course it is not true to say that Britain had complete dominance over all sea traffic in the Mediterranean, a number of Axis cargoes obviously got through to North Africa and a number of British convoys were attacked in turn, but matters got progressively worse for Rommel as Montgomery's army pushed westwards. In the period following Alamein, Eighth Army's advance opened up more and more airfields along the coast of North Africa from which to harass even further these Axis convoys.

The most pressing problem facing Rommel as he retreated westwards through Libya was the quality of his supply lines. Whilst it was true that the farther he travelled, the closer he came to the ports from which he obtained most of his provisions – Tobruk, Benghazi, Tripoli – Eighth Army was always close on his heels forcing him to give them up no sooner than he arrived. It seemed to him that there could be no respite until he reached a stable defence line such as that at Mareth just inside Tunisia. Here he could at least strengthen a position from which he could make a stand and stop Eighth Army's inexorable progress whilst his masters in Rome and Berlin sorted out a proper strategy for the North African theatre.

For Montgomery the victory at Alamein was everything that he had hoped for. Rommel had been soundly beaten by an overwhelming force which even after the battle showed no signs of diminishing; in fact it was growing in strength with each new convoy that arrived in Egypt along the 'safe' route around the Cape of Good Hope. Montgomery could face his future with equanimity, sound in the knowledge that a new Anglo-American army was about to arrive in North Africa and help squeeze the Desert Fox in a new trap.

BRITISH PLANS

General Montgomery's intentions after Alamein were to force Panzerarmee Afrika into total retreat and to try to overwhelm its surviving numbers in battle. He expected that during his retreat Rommel would use various old defence lines to make some sort of stand. These locations had seen previous battles in the to-and-fro nature of the desert war; names that recalled earlier triumphs on both sides, such as Tobruk, Gazala, Mersa Matruh and El Agheila. Montgomery respected Rommel's reputation and was determined not to allow him to turn on him suddenly from one of these positions and catch him off guard. Eighth Army's commander was resolute in his decision that every time an enemy defence position blocked his way, he would always attack it with a set-piece assault of great strength. Unlike Rommel, he would never try to 'bounce' a position through surprise or unorthodox manoeuvre. Montgomery would ensure there was no chance of suffering a setback for he now had his victorious reputation to think of.

LEFT
During the pursuit across Egypt and into Libya, everything required to keep Eighth Army supplied during the chase had to be lorried forwards on trucks. The scale of this logistic exercise was enormous as was the prodigious amount of fuel necessary to keep just the transport rolling. (DA-00937, War History Collection, Alexander Turnbull Library, Wellington NZ)

RIGHT
Transport south-east of Mersa Matruh prior to dispersal. The broken nature of the terrain can be seen in the foreground. The going was always very difficult for trucks once they had to abandon the main coastal road. (DA-02551, War History Collection, Alexander Turnbull Library, Wellington NZ)

LEFT
A German 88mm anti-aircraft battery from 19. Flak-Division had been trying to escape off the road into the desert but was destroyed by the guns of Eighth Army. (IWM, NA1619)

RIGHT
After Eighth Army left the flat featureless landscape of Libya and Egypt behind, it exchanged desert sands for the undulating hills and valleys of Tunisia. (IWM, NA1425)

Across North Africa one defence line stood out as being stronger than any other, that at Mareth in Tunisia. At the time of Alamein this line had been virtually demilitarized, for Tunisia was a colony of the Vichy French government which had signed a pact with the Axis powers. On 8 November, when Anglo-American forces landed in Algeria and prepared to move on Tunis, the strategic picture changed. The Germans flooded men and equipment into Tunisia and eventually formed an army there. The Mareth Line suddenly became important again, this time for the Axis.

Eighth Army's original plan of attack at the Mareth Line was relatively straightforward. It would begin with an initial frontal assault, followed by a massive armoured exploitation, hoping to win through with overwhelming force. Monty also envisaged using the New Zealand Division for one of its flanking attacks which were now becoming a feature of the campaign. The New Zealanders would try to make a sweeping movement behind the Matmata Hills to emerge in the rear of the Italian–German forces manning the defence line. The move would either cut off their retreat and isolate them, or cause them to fall back to the next defence line based around Wadi Akarit.

By the time this attack could be made, Tunisia would have become an Anglo-American theatre after the *Torch* landings in Morocco and Algeria. North Africa would no longer be Eighth Army's 'show'. Montgomery would have to share the limelight with the newcomers and Alexander's options as British C.-in-C. Middle East would have to take into account American views and Eisenhower's authority. Eighth Army's plans had to be dovetailed into Allied strategic objectives. This would be to the benefit of both armies for each attack could be timed to put the Axis forces at a disadvantage.

Just prior to Monty's assault on the Mareth Line, it was decided that the Americans would use their II Corps, under the command of Maj. Gen. George Patton, to tie up German units to the rear of the Mareth positions by moving out of their lodgement in the south-east of Tunisia against El Guettar and Maknassy and so threaten the enemy's ability to withdraw back along the coast through Gabes. This two-pronged operation would not be mutually supportive as the gap between the British and Americans was still very much enemy territory, but it was hoped that with both the front and the rear of Messe's Italian–German Army under threat, it would be required to withdraw ever northward. This would shrink the enemy's front into what would eventually become a bottleneck, which could then be squeezed into a small pocket ripe for annihilation.

AXIS PLANS

After the collapse at El Alamein, Rommel's main hope was simply to survive. As he retreated from the battlefield he and his army were constantly in great danger of destruction and capture. As was to be expected, the British immediately turned from attack into pursuit, trying to gear up their advance into a purely mobile operation. All that Rommel and his scattered forces could do was to flee. For the first few weeks of the escape, the main priority was to gain time on his pursuers.

The poor state of Panzerarmee Afrika meant that it would be no longer possible to stand and fight. It did still have some sting in its tail with its surviving Panzers and a few anti-tank guns and was often able to turn on the advance guards of Eighth Army for a short while and give them a fright. Indeed, Rommel's masters in Berlin and Rome continually urged him to stand and fight, but he knew that his army was in no fit state to do so. He made pretence of withdrawing to defensive positions in his rear to make a stand, but he knew that it would not be possible to hold any of them until his army had been reinforced, replenished and revitalized.

On 8 November 1942, just a few days after the end at Alamein, everything changed for Rommel and for the whole Axis strategy. The *Torch* landings in Algeria and Morocco and the following Allied move into Tunisia resulted in the need for a new Axis army to be raised to counter them. Over the next few months supplies and reinforcements were shipped across to North Africa, most of which were not destined for the benefit of Rommel, although some

These signs on the outskirts of Sirte give warning that the retreating enemy has left booby traps everywhere. Best for everyone if they just kept well clear of the town until the engineers had cleared them. Demolitions and booby traps were a constant threat during the advance and claimed the lives of many unwary soldiers and civilians. (IWM, E21279)

of this new *matériel* was sent eastwards to aid him, but instead for Arnim's new 5. Panzerarmee Afrika that was being raised in Tunisia.

With two Axis armies in North Africa, neither of which could match those of the Allies, it was possible to consider a new strategy for the region. Hitler agreed with fellow dictator Benito Mussolini that Tunisia would be held for as long as possible. With the fate of Libya in the balance, it now became critical that an Italian–German presence remained along the southern Mediterranean coast. If both Libya and Tunisia fell to the Allies, Axis maritime traffic would be totally confined to the northern parts of the Mediterranean away from Allied airbases. This must not be allowed to happen.

As Rommel was pushed farther and farther westwards by British Eighth Army, he was continually looking over his shoulder at his bases in his rear. More and more he thought that only two options were possible: either a complete withdrawal from North Africa, or a retreat into Tunisia to join up with Arnim's army, both of which meant giving up the whole of Libya. Hitler immediately vetoed the first option; the second became inevitable in the face of Montgomery's superior forces. However, once he was inside the Tunisian border and safely behind the Mareth defence line, he knew that it would take weeks for Eighth Army to be in a position to launch an attack. This respite might give him some flexibility over his next move.

Unfortunately for Rommel, most of his plans, his supply situation and his arguments with his masters were all known to the British. The cryptographers at Station X at Bletchley Park in England were regularly breaking the German Enigma codes. The interception of many of the dispatches sent by radio between Rome, Berlin and North Africa, resulted in the British always being one step ahead of Rommel. The results of the decoding were forwarded to Monty and his team as soon as the enemy messages could be interpreted. Not every transmission could be decoded, and it often took several days to interpret just one message, but enough German communications were read to make the process extremely useful. It was not just a simple case of listening in and writing the message down; the whole process was very complicated. Often an important opportunity was missed by the delay. However, even if surprise attacks could not be launched nor traps sprung to take advantage of the information gained, the process gave a great insight into German military strategy and tactics and of the gradual breakdown in Rommel's health and morale. Montgomery was able to see just how considerable Rommel's problems were and just what the German field marshal intended to do about them.

The defence of the Mareth Line would put Rommel in a position that went against his natural abilities. He was a master of manoeuvre and to be tied down behind fixed defences was anathema to him. Although he knew that the strength of his forces, especially in armour, would never match those of Eighth Army and that defence was the only possible option open to him, he still harboured the thought of striking at the British from out of the minefields and bunkers of the Mareth Line. A sudden attack could well panic Montgomery's army and give his beleaguered forces more time.

When Rommel's forces arrived in Tunisia close to those of Arnim's, thought could be given to exchanging formations between the two commands. With Panzerarmee Afrika on the Mareth Line and the probability of a period of static warfare, one of the Afrika Korps' Panzer formations, 21. Panzer-Division, could be transferred to the sector facing Allied First Army. This prompted Rommel to consider going on the offensive and using it to attack the American front.

THE PURSUIT AFTER EL ALAMEIN

The crushing blow delivered by Operation *Supercharge* at the end of the Alamein battle threw Rommel's forces into a state of confusion. Everywhere on the battlefield Axis units were struggling to extricate themselves from the fighting and withdraw. Rommel knew it was the end and gave instructions for an organized retreat, with Italian formations being the first to pull out. When Hitler heard of the move he immediately countermanded the order. Rommel could do nothing but comply, rescinding his previous instructions and ordering all units to stand firm. The result was a disorganized mess; some formations were pulling out westwards as other units were trying to resume a defensive stand looking eastwards. Communication became disjointed and all focus lost. The defeated troops cowering under a continual bombardment by Eighth Army's guns all wanted to know, were they staying to die fighting or were they pulling out to fight another day?

The agony Rommel was forced to endure after receiving the Führer's order not to retreat was eased late on 4 November when Hitler, realizing that the battle had been well and truly lost, relented and allowed the field marshal to pull back to a new defensive line at Fuka. Before he received this news Rommel had already set a retreat in motion, rescinding the order to remain and fight and giving new orders for a general withdrawal. Generalfeldmarschall Kesselring had come over from Rome to his headquarters to see the situation for himself and had agreed that all Axis forces would have to retreat or risk complete destruction. That evening, after much delay, 70,000 survivors of the battle were all trying to head west, some along the coast road whilst others trekked across the desert.

The end of the battle of Alamein had left both sides in a state of chaos, but Montgomery hoped to cut through this confusion and get his mobile formations after the enemy as quickly as possible. He ordered Lt. Gen. Freyberg to take the New Zealand Division and 4th Light Armoured Brigade in a large sweeping movement to bypass Rommel's rearguard and make for Fuka. It was here that Eighth Army intended to cut the coast road and corner the retreating enemy. In the meantime, Lt. Gen. Lumsden's X Corps would use its armour to make shorter envelopments to trap and annihilate those forces caught between the New Zealand manoeuvre and the sea, whilst Lt. Gen. Leese's XXX Corps maintained its relentless pressure on those of Rommel's forces still on the battlefield. Lieutenant-General Horrocks' XIII Corps would clean up and deal with the thousands of Axis infantry, mainly Italian, who had been captured or left behind.

The opportunity of exploiting Rommel's demise through a rapid drive westwards by strong armoured forces did not get off to a good start. The initial moves soon began to degenerate into a mêlée of tanks and vehicles all trying to squeeze through the narrow portal that had been opened through the German minefields by Operation *Supercharge*. Too many tanks and not enough room to manoeuvre slowed the start of the chase. The New Zealand Division was also delayed waiting for the arrival of 4th Light Armoured Brigade from the rear of the battlefield. Vital hours were lost concentrating Freyberg's force and little progress was made before darkness fell and units closed up until morning. The armoured divisions of X Corps making the shorter flanking movement towards the coast ran into pockets of enemy resistance and had to fight small actions before pressing on.

Montgomery hoped that on 5 November the New Zealand force would be at Fuka to close the door on Rommel's route westwards trapping the better part of his motorized units. At the same time Lumsden's tanks from 1st and 7th Armoured Divisions would be pounding the coast road and harrying Axis forces speeding towards the Fuka bottleneck. To ease congestion, X Corps directed 10th Armoured Division to make for a point farther to the west of Fuka to deal with those of the enemy who had already managed to avoid being trapped. All of these sweeping movements were intended to hit the demoralized Panzerarmee Afrika in its flank from out of the desert.

As it turned out, the events of 5 November were far from what Eighth Army's commander had intended: the New Zealand Division failed to reach Fuka in time having been held up by a dummy minefield short of its objective; 10th Armoured Division lost its way and turned north too soon to arrive on the coast road well short of Fuka; 1st Armoured Division was held up by enemy rearguards only 32km into its advance and 7th Armoured Division which had been re-routed farther west because of 10th Armoured's loss of direction, was held up on the same dummy minefield as Lt. Gen. Freyberg's New Zealanders. The result was that the trap was not closed and Rommel's main forces escaped from what should have been certain destruction.

The immediate aftermath of El Alamein

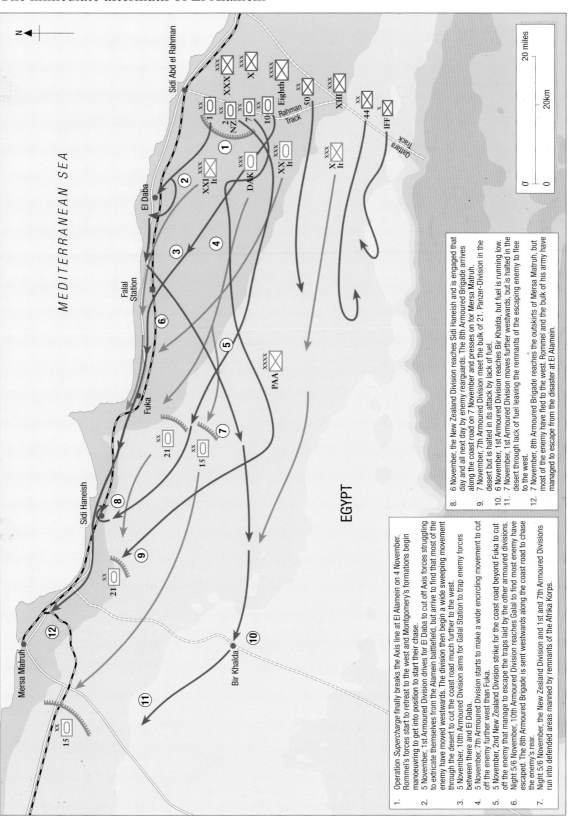

1. Operation *Supercharge* finally breaks the Axis line at El Alamein on 4 November. Rommel's forces start to retreat to the west and Montgomery's formations begin manoeuvring to get into position to start their chase.
2. 5 November, 1st Armoured Division drives for El Daba to cut off Axis forces struggling to extricate themselves from the Alamein battlefield, but arrive to find that most of the enemy have moved westwards. The division then begin a wide sweeping movement through the desert to cut the coast road much further to the west.
3. 5 November, 10th Armoured Division aims for Galal Station to trap enemy forces between there and El Daba.
4. 5 November, 7th Armoured Division starts to make a wide encircling movement to cut off the enemy further west than Fuka.
5. 5 November, 2nd New Zealand Division strike for the coast road beyond Fuka to cut off the enemy that manage to escape the traps laid by the other armoured divisions.
6. Night 5/6 November, 10th Armoured Division reaches Galal to find most enemy have escaped. The 8th Armoured Brigade is sent westwards along the coast road to chase the enemy's rear.
7. Night 5/6 November, the New Zealand Division and 1st and 7th Armoured Divisions run into defended areas manned by remnants of the Afrika Korps.
8. 6 November, the New Zealand Division reaches Sidi Haneish and is engaged that day and all next day by enemy rearguards. The 8th Armoured Brigade arrives along the coast road on 7 November and presses on for Mersa Matruh.
9. 7 November, 7th Armoured Division meet the bulk of 21. Panzer-Division in the desert but is halted in its attack by lack of fuel.
10. 6 November, 1st Armoured Division reaches Bir Khalda, but fuel is running low.
11. 7 November, 1st Armoured Division moves further westwards, but is halted in the desert through lack of fuel leaving the remnants of the escaping enemy to flee to the west.
12. 7 November, 8th Armoured Brigade reaches the outskirts of Mersa Matruh, but most of the enemy have fled to the west. Rommel and the bulk of his army have managed to escape from the disaster at El Alamein.

The rain that marred the initial stages of the pursuit turned the desert floor into a soggy quagmire. Even four-wheel-drive trucks moved with great difficulty. (DA-12876, War History Collection, Alexander Turnbull Library, Wellington NZ)

Lieutenant-General Lumsden was later criticized for the slow nature of X Corps' chase. He had allowed his force to cut the coast road too soon in tight manoeuvres which enabled much of the enemy force to get to the west of him, rather than making the wider sweeps to catch the bulk of it around Fuka. Freyberg was also criticized for his lack of drive in taking Fuka. Monty himself was later also censured by historians for allowing the results of his great victory at Alamein to be devalued by his failure to ensure the complete destruction of his beaten enemy. Few of Eighth Army's commanders escaped criticism from later historians regarding their performance on the days following Alamein.

With so much hostile armour pressing at their heels and with RAF fighter-bombers strafing the tightly packed columns of transport streaming westwards, Rommel's forces were unable to organize a defensive position on the improvised line at Fuka and continued to pull back hoping to make some sort of stand at Mersa Matruh. On 6 November Montgomery's pursuit started to get more organized and it looked as though the motorized units of the New Zealand and 7th Armoured Divisions would beat the enemy to Mersa Matruh, but delays and their reluctance to advance by night saw them both fail. Fuel and water became scarcer as supply lines lengthened and then the weather intervened. Heavy rainfall reduced the desert floor to a soggy morass. Tanks and vehicles floundered in the mud and all aerial support was grounded. In growing frustration Eighth Army laboured through the quagmire of the desert whilst its enemy ground his way westwards along the coastal highway. Rommel decided to abandon the Mersa Matruh position after no more than token resistance by a small rearguard and continued his retreat up onto the Sollum Heights overlooking the Egypt–Libya border.

The only two roads over the mountainous region passed through narrow defiles along routes hampered by tortuous hairpin bends. The road near the coast at Sollum was expertly cratered by German engineers and made impassable immediately after the bulk of Axis traffic had passed through. The other road, 8km to the south, crossed over the Halfaya Pass and was kept open for any stragglers that managed the climb up the twisting road that led to the top. The pass itself was heavily defended by Italian infantry ensconced in concrete emplacements or dug in around the summit. Rommel planned to employ no more than delaying tactics on the Sollum Heights, holding the hills just long enough to withdraw the main part of his forces into new positions around Tobruk. Behind him he left small groups of engineers sowing dummy minefields strewn with buried scrap metal and laying booby traps of all kinds to slow down the pursuing British.

The responsibility of opening the Halfaya Pass was given to the infantry of the New Zealand Division. Freyberg chose his 21st Battalion for the task and urged the attack to go in immediately the unit had reached Halfaya. Just before dawn on 11 November, Lt. Col. Harding led his men into the attack. It was a very brief affair for the now-isolated Italians had little left to fight for. Over their shoulders they could see the dust thrown up by their comrades and their allies as they fled across the plain towards the west, all hastening to put as much distance as they could between themselves and Eighth Army. The New Zealanders stormed the pass and the Italians, where they could, threw up their arms. The cost of the battle amounted to one New Zealander killed and one wounded, with between 60 and 70 killed and wounded on the Italian side and just over 600 men captured.

Montgomery's forces could now look down over the border into Libya and see the last of their quarry fleeing westwards. Rommel and his desert army had got away. The defeated Axis forces were no longer a hemmed-in, disorganized, beaten rabble struggling for their very survival. They were now able to spread out, reorganize, consolidate and defend. They were still in a very precarious position, their strength was poor and they had constantly to look to their rear for safety, but at least they now had their enemy at arm's length, and for every kilometre they travelled westwards their supply lines, poor as they were, shortened, whilst those of Eighth Army lengthened. Defeat

A New Zealand column climbing up the Halfaya Pass in Egypt during the pursuit. The congestion was so great that vehicles often had to wait for hours before securing a chance to ascend. (DA- 06745, War History Collection, Alexander Turnbull Library, Wellington NZ)

AXIS FORCES IN FULL RETREAT AFTER THE BATTLE OF EL ALAMEIN (pp. 32–33)

The defeat of Rommel's Panzerarmee Afrika was so complete that most of the withdrawal from the battlefield was a rout. Those German units which could be gathered together by their commanders retreated in some order using whatever transport was available, but the Italian formations were left to make their own exit in any way possible.

Most of the Italian divisions had few vehicles of their own. They had been used primarily as static formations, brought into the line for the purposes of defence and then left. When the end came they were simply abandoned with no means of escape except on foot **(1)**. After the collapse the desert was covered by demoralized Italian troops all shuffling westwards until they were overtaken by the British and ordered back into POW cages. A few lucky ones commandeered the odd lorry and tried to escape along the coast road, but here they were at the mercy of the marauding fighters of the RAF.

The truck **(2)** is a Fiat Spa Dovunque 3 ton, which was a six-wheeled troop carrier, with rear four-wheeled drive. It has been hit by a low-flying interceptor which has caused it to be abandoned. One man lies dead by the side of the road whilst its surviving passengers contemplate their fate. Tired and dejected they await the arrival of their victorious enemy and their exit from the war. To add to their discomfort, tanks of their German ally speed past away from the pursuing British without even a sideways glance.

The tanks **(3)** of the fleeing Panzer divisions have escaped from Montgomery's final entrapment and are trying to join up with the rest of their unit in the west, hoping to form a stop line somewhere between El Daba and Mersa Matruh. They have chosen to try to make haste along the coast road, but are in danger of falling victim to the strafing tactics of the RAF. In the background many of their comrades have fallen victim to the heavy cannons of Hurricane fighters and have left burning hulks scattered across the desert **(4)**. Most tanks chose to spread out and make slower progress across the rough ground of the open desert, rather than use the quicker, but often congested, highway.

was still a possibility, but they had now evaded the complete annihilation that they had feared just a week before.

Back in Egypt, Montgomery was smothered in praise over the victory he had masterminded at Alamein. News quickly arrived that he had been promoted to full general. The nation rejoiced, his army's morale was sky high and he was already putting pen to paper to educate future commanders about how he thought future battles ought to be fought. This praise was, however, a little premature for he had failed in one of the great tenets of warfare – an enemy beaten on the battlefield should be resolutely pursued and destroyed. Montgomery had let Rommel get away.

In Tobruk, the remnants of Panzerarmee Afrika were arriving back in small groups readying themselves for a siege just like that endured by Eighth Army earlier that year. Some units, most notably the Italians, were sent back farther to the east to work on reinforcing the positions around El Agheila and Mersa Brega, the old defence line from which Rommel had launched his first offensive against the British almost two years before.

Everyone thought that Rommel would try to hold out at Tobruk until reinforced. Indeed, Italian high command insisted that he did, ordering him not to give up one more metre of Libyan soil; Mussolini was desperate to hold on to his North African colony. Rommel himself knew that it would be hopeless to do so for he had neither the troops to garrison the port nor the means of resupplying them. He knew that the advancing British would use their overwhelming strength to encircle the area from the landward side and capture the city with relative ease. He gave the order to evacuate Tobruk and head to the rear.

The arrival of Allied forces in Tunisia made Rommel even more determined to pull back as far as possible, leaving the whole of Cyrenaica, including the ports of Tobruk and Benghazi, to the British. He outwardly gave every indication that he would make a stand at El Agheila, but at the same time lobbied Hitler for permission to move farther westwards towards Tunisia to join up with the growing number of German forces arriving there. He went further and suggested that the campaign in North Africa was now a hopeless enterprise and all Axis forces should be evacuated by sea and the whole continent abandoned. Not surprisingly Hitler was outraged at such defeatist talk and ordered Rommel to fight on. Politically, Hitler could do little else, for if Italy was forced to abandon the last of its colonial territories in Africa, Mussolini and his fascist government would in all probability fall.

At 0900hrs on 13 November the lorried infantry of 131st Infantry Brigade entered Tobruk followed by the main body of 7th Armoured Division. The 4th Light Armoured Brigade then pushed on along the coast road making for the old front line at Gazala. An armoured column was sent southwards to scout towards Bir Hacheim to ensure none of Rommel's forces was at large in the desert. The main part of the armoured brigade brushed up against some strong resistance at Gazala and was brought to action, but the confrontation was no more than a stiff skirmish for the enemy soon retreated to join up with the main force. Brigadier Harvey's brigade then pushed on towards Derna and the Martuba airfields which were reached on 15 November. It was becoming increasingly clear that Rommel was intent on falling back to the El Agheila Line where the British had been rebuffed on two previous occasions. This natural defensive position was known to the British as El Agheila and to the Axis forces as Mersa Brega, their names derived from the two locations along the coast between which the defences lay.

The Germans had demolished all the facilities at Tobruk and the port was not immediately available for use. For the moment Eighth Army's supplies had to continue being lorried forwards from dumps inside Egypt, whilst engineers and the Royal Navy worked feverishly to clear the harbour. Supplies to keep the whole of Eighth Army in the pursuit were not available and Montgomery now had to decide what forces were required to continue the chase and what formations were to be left behind.

X Corps had been responsible up to now for the advance and Montgomery decided that it should continue with 7th Armoured Division and 2nd New Zealand Division, supported by 4th Light Armoured Brigade under command. Lieutenant-General Oliver Leese's XXX Corps would take over later and plan for the set-piece battle that was expected to be fought at El Agheila.

Aerial reconnaissance now indicated that Panzerarmee Afrika was also giving up Benghazi without a fight, albeit only after the port itself was destroyed. Rommel was continuing his retreat, making for the natural defensive position between Mersa Brega and El Agheila. His formations were using the long route along the coast road. This left the way open for a dash through the desert via Mecheli and Msus by British armoured forces, just as Lt. Gen. Richard O'Connor had done in 1940 and Gen. Claude Auchinleck in 1941. It was now suggested that a relatively small but powerful force could cut across the desert and close the coast road before El Agheila to trap as much of the enemy as possible.

Montgomery would not hear of the move; he was cautious about exposing his army to any kind of setback. He did not want to experience the kind of counterattack that had been launched by the enemy twice before, even though

British sappers working hard to repair the coastal highway after German engineers had done their best to make it impassable during their retreat. (IWM, E21790)

aerial reconnaissance and secret intelligence from Ultra intercepts proved that the enemy had only 30 tanks and 20 armoured cars, and his artillery had been reduced to 46 anti-tank and 40 88mm guns. Montgomery insisted that his main force would advance along the coast road in Rommel's wake and prepare itself for a set-piece battle at El Agheila. A column of armoured cars did attempt the desert route, but its advance was slowed by rainstorms which washed out desert tracks.

The last of Panzerarmee Afrika pulled out of Benghazi on 19 November and by nightfall had reached Agedabia. Three days later its forces were inside the defensive line at El Agheila. The British armoured car column did manage to swing through the desert and reach the coast road between Agedabia and Benghazi on the 20th, but found the highway empty and the enemy flown. Those of Rommel's army that had survived the battle at El Alamein had now retreated some 1,300km in just over three weeks, fighting rearguard actions and husbanding fuel and ammunition to arrive into prepared positions in which to regain strength. On paper they were in a lamentable state, but their fighting reputation was still formidable enough to force their opponents to treat them with great caution.

In contrast to all the problems facing Rommel, Montgomery was in top form. He was in complete control of the situation. The long lines of communications from Egypt to El Agheila of course caused some difficulties, but they were at least capable of being resolved. The commander of Eighth Army was confident of ultimate success. Slowly, surely and with great strength he would grind down all Axis forces. Montgomery was not interested in bouncing the enemy positions at El Agheila with a sudden rush; he would attack only when he was sure of victory with overwhelming force.

A British 6-pdr anti-tank gun and its attendant carriers seems to have come to grief near a road block. (IWM, NA1482)

Eighth Army's arrival opposite the El Agheila–Mersa Brega line now allowed Montgomery to concentrate on planning the set-piece battle he would launch to clear them. Even though observed intelligence and secret Ultra decrypts were showing that his enemy was in no fit state to hold the line with more than just a token resistance, he was taking no chances. Montgomery now had an immense reputation to preserve and was not willing to allow any setbacks. But first there was a need to reorganize his army.

With his forces spread across 1,300km of North Africa, Montgomery's immediate concerns related to his supplies and administration, rather than battles and pursuit. The stretched-out nature of his advance meant that he no longer needed three corps in action. It would be less strain on his administration if one of them was disbanded and its formations dispersed. He decided to dispense with XIII Corps and move its commander, Lt. Gen. Brian Horrocks, across to X Corps to replace Lt. Gen. Lumsden whose recent performance at the start of the pursuit had been found to be poor. The divisions of XIII Corps were given new roles; 44th Infantry Division was disbanded and 50th and 4th Indian Divisions were held in GHQ reserve with the intention of joining XXX Corps later in the campaign.

Montgomery's carefully prepared attack on El Agheila was planned to start on the night of 16–17 December. On 26 November Lt. Gen. Leese and his XXX Corps took over the forward area from X Corps. The corps now comprised 7th Armoured, 51st (Highland) and the New Zealand Divisions. The plan was for X Corps to withdraw to the Benghazi area to act as a reserve in the event that Rommel staged one of his remarkable comebacks.

Montgomery's plan of attack was conventional. He decided on a frontal assault near the coast by 51st and 7th Armoured Divisions to pin down the defences, whilst a wide sweep through the desert to the south by the New Zealand Division would get behind the line and seal Rommel's forces in a trap. The Desert Air Force would support these attacks and be ready to deal with any sudden retreat by Axis forces.

Rommel had for some time realized that his so-called defensive line at El Agheila was in fact indefensible. It stretched for almost 160km out into the desert, longer even than his line at El Alamein, and he had neither the troops nor the supplies to man it. Most of his heavy weapons and anti-tank guns had been left on the battlefield at Alamein and the bulk of his armour destroyed. His fuel situation showed little chance of improving now that Arnim was raising a new army in Tunisia and also needed supplies. Over the coming days, however, a trickle of reinforcements did arrive along with a few replacements tanks.

Rommel knew that his holding of the line at El Agheila would eventually lead to his army's destruction and began to ask the Italian chief in Rome, Maresciallo Cavallero, for permission to engage in a further withdrawal to at least Buerat or even Tripoli. Here supplies of fuel, water, ammunition and reinforcements could be fed straight into the line from the port. His supply lines would shorten by some 400km whilst Montgomery's would extend by the same amount.

Maresciallo Cavallero rejected Rommel's proposition as being intolerable, for Mussolini had decreed that there was to be no further retreat in Libya. This decision was later ratified by Berlin; Rommel was to stand and fight at El Agheila. Hitler did, however, promise that more guns and tanks would soon arrive. He also reminded Rommel that he came under the command of the Italian governor of Libya, Maresciallo Bastico, and had to obey his orders.

Rommel now began pestering Bastico with details of the plight of Panzerarmee Afrika, warning him that ultimately North Africa could not be held. Messages passed back and forth between Libya and Rome and matters reached a head when the three field marshals, Bastico, Cavallero and Kesselring, agreed to meet with Rommel. The conference took place in the desert at the triumphant arch (Arco dei Fileni) that Mussolini had built in 1930 to celebrate his entry into Cyrenaica. Known to the British as Marble Arch, the monument was the setting for some heated discussion. Rommel was forceful in his opinion that the line at El Agheila would be impossible to hold against strong opposition with the forces he had. A sweeping movement through the desert in the south by British armour would ensure that his positions were outflanked in a matter of days. The other three commanders disagreed with him and insisted, through a combination of flattery and threat, that Rommel could and should hold the line and stop the British advance.

Emboldened by support from his superiors, Bastico even went so far as to order counterattacks to be made on the British advance guards arriving in the area. He also told Rommel that he was forbidden to sanction any further withdrawal without his permission. Undaunted by Bastico's overbearing outburst, the very next day Rommel turned to Gen. Navarini, Commander Italian XXI Corpo, and asked him to prepare for a further retreat by his infantry to Buerat.

Rommel was obviously suffering under a great deal of pressure both from his bosses in Rome and from the situation on the battlefield. After two years in the desert, his health was beginning to fail. He was plagued by a skin complaint; he suffered from relentless headaches and, in a letter to his wife, admitted that his nerves were 'shot to pieces'. The relentless strain now caused him to make a very rash decision. He was sure that if Hitler was presented with a complete picture of the situation in North Africa he would relent and allow a retreat to take place either to Tripoli or farther westwards into Tunisia to meet up with Arnim. He decided to go to see the Führer in person.

Without the knowledge of his superiors or permission from the theatre commander, Rommel took himself off to Rastenburg in East Prussia to plead his case. When he arrived at Hitler's headquarters the Führer was appalled by his action. 'How dare you leave your command without my permission?' he demanded. A heated discussion then took place in which Hitler berated Rommel for his defeatist attitude and for trying to suggest that a complete withdrawal from North Africa was the only possible solution. He was tired of his generals advocating retreats and ordered Rommel to stay and fight it out to the last man.

Hitler could see that his favourite general was obviously ill and was beginning to lack resolve. As a concession he promised that the Luftwaffe would help out with the supply situation by airlifting as much forwards as possible. Rommel eventually returned to Libya with an even greater sense of hopelessness, but continued pressing Kesselring and his superiors in Rome for some easing of their intransigence. The doctrine of holding fast just for the sake of it was militarily unsound; he desperately needed a more coherent strategy that reflected Montgomery's growing strength and his increasing weakness. Unfortunately, this continual whinging by Rommel only hardened his superiors' attitudes and a consensus began to arise that his removal from the theatre might be a good thing. However, on 1 December Mussolini did relent to the point of allowing Rommel to pull back to Buerat if it appeared the position at El Agheila would be lost to a British attack.

A convoy of tanks and vehicles belonging to 1st Armoured Division has been hit by marauding Luftwaffe fighters during the advance into Tunisia. (IWM, NA1794)

Rommel had no intention of losing any men or equipment on the lines at Mersa Brega and El Agheila. He knew that Montgomery was massing for the attack and he was determined not to be pinned down by fighting a defensive battle. On 6 December he signalled Navarini to begin pulling out his Italian infantry that night and to start the retreat to Buerat. This was done over the next two nights completely unnoticed by the British. The lines were then lightly held by just German troops and the Italian Divisione Corrazzata 'Ariete' which Rommel intended to withdraw just moments before the British attack, leaving Eighth Army's artillery bombardment to fall on an empty front line sown with just mines and booby traps.

On 10 December increasing activity by the British indicated that their attack was imminent. They had finally spotted the earlier withdrawals and knew that Rommel was now intending to pull out of the line. To counter this, Montgomery brought the start date for his attack forwards by 48 hours to the night of 14–15 December. To the south of the line, German aerial reconnaissance soon showed that British armoured cars and armour were in the desert scouting forwards working a way around Rommel's flank. On 13 December this activity increased and just before midnight a heavy artillery barrage began. Rommel instinctively knew that it was now time for the motorized forces to pull out.

Eighth Army moved forwards into the attack as planned but was slowed almost to a standstill by minefields, demolitions and booby traps and by skilful rearguard actions by the 'Ariete' Division. The New Zealand Division also made its flanking movement through the desert as planned, although with much difficulty due to lack of fuel, but when it reached the coast road it found that once again the enemy had flown.

The advance from Benghazi to Tripoli

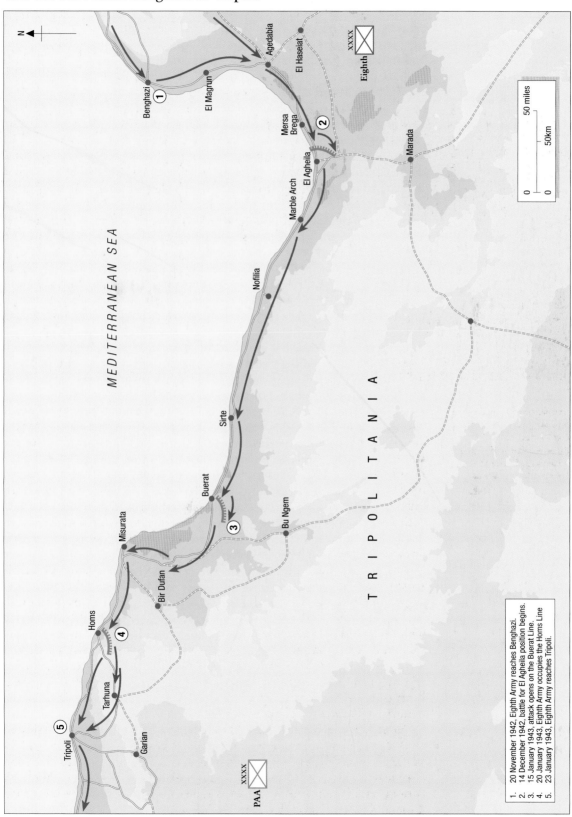

N

MEDITERRANEAN SEA

TRIPOLITANIA

Benghazi ①
El Magrun
Agedabia
El Haselat
Mersa Brega
②
El Agheila
Marble Arch
Marada
Nofilia
Sirte
Buerat
③
Bu Ngem
Misurata
Bir Dufan
Homs ④
Tarhuna
⑤
Tripoli
Garian

XXXX Eighth

XXXX PAA

0   50 miles
0   50km

1. 20 November 1942, Eighth Army reaches Benghazi.
2. 14 December 1942, battle for El Agheila position begins.
3. 15 January 1943, attack opens on the Buerat Line.
4. 20 January 1943, Eighth Army occupies the Homs Line
5. 23 January 1943, Eighth Army reaches Tripoli.

The Axis withdrawal to Buerat was marked by fuel shortages and harassment from the air. The coast road became littered with burnt-out vehicles and more than once Rommel himself had to dive for cover from low-flying fighter-bombers. Behind him intricate booby traps, demolitions and mines slowed the pursuers along the main road. Much of the British armour and transport was forced to make detours into the desert to shadow the Axis retreat and then make sudden turns northwards to try to catch their enemy in the flank. Rearguards fought skilful actions with the British when they pressed too close and whenever Rommel's men were in danger of being surrounded, they broke into small groups and made their escape.

Panzerarmee Afrika made it into the Buerat position with most of the force that left Mersa Brega intact. It did not take Rommel long before he realized that he had exchanged one exposed untenable defence line for another. Once again he lobbied Rome for permission to make a further withdrawal and once again it was refused with bitter recriminations. Kesselring, Cavallero and Mussolini all agreed that Rommel's mental stability was suspect and that he was convinced that retreat was the only safe option. Again and again they urged him to make a stand, even though he reminded them that all the British had to do was drive through the desert round his flanks and catch his army in a trap. Rommel was supported in his opinions by his Italian commanders who urged him to arrange the evacuation of his 45,000 infantry westwards whilst there was still time.

Bastico complained that the German commander was interested only in getting to Tunisia in the fastest possible time. Kesselring came over to Africa and met with Rommel again and urged him to use what force he had to make it difficult for the British. His situation might be bad, but Montgomery's forces were also in a precarious position. Their supply lines were so stretched that they could not possibly attack the Buerat Line for some weeks. Further meetings with the other two field marshals degenerated into rows. The senior commanders all agreed that it might be best for Rommel to be replaced some time in the future by an Italian commander and for him to be returned to Germany for a rest. Reluctantly they agreed that without the means or intention of holding Eighth Army it was inevitable that Tripoli would be lost. They gave permission for Rommel to initiate a further withdrawal to the area of Homs just short of Tripoli if his force was threatened with complete destruction. He would then hold the British in front of Tripoli whilst the port was destroyed. He was further ordered to delay the British as long as possible during any retreat; two clear months must pass before he could withdraw into the defences of the Mareth Line.

After the El Agheila action Montgomery held court to explain to the world how he had once again outwitted Rommel, 'hustling' him out of a strong defensive line by overwhelming force of arms. The 'battle' of El Agheila demonstrated to him that Rommel's army was no longer the power it once was, nor could it ever be again. The *Torch* landings and the increasing numbers of airfields all along the Mediterranean coast allowed the seaways to become more secure for the Allies and more dangerous for the enemy. It was out of the question that Rommel's forces could be rebuilt to a point where they could go on the offensive again. Montgomery knew that a strong, cautious advance into Tunisia would inevitably result in complete victory for him.

Rommel stayed on the Buerat Line throughout December and into the new year (1943). Opposite him Eighth Army gathered ready to launch another massive attack. Montgomery knew that Rommel would not remain at Buerat any longer than necessary, but would employ the usual delaying tactics to prevent Eighth Army advancing too close to his tail. Monty therefore expanded the plan for the Buerat attack in order to take in both the battle itself and a rapid exploitation towards Tripoli. He ensured that all formations had the means to continue the advance without pause and to be in the Libyan capital in ten days. The attack was to be launched by XXX Corps on 15 January with 50th and 51st Divisions advancing along the coast road and 7th Armoured and the New Zealand Divisions attacking parallel but well inland. The 23rd Armoured Brigade covered the ground between and acted as a link between the formations. This plan was later modified after a storm hit the port of Benghazi on 3 January and badly affected the build-up of supplies. The 50th Division was withdrawn from the plan in order to conserve supplies.

With little new fuel or supplies reaching him to help reinforce his defence of the Buerat Line, Rommel had started the long task of withdrawing those formations without transport early in January. For the next week just German forces held the line. By 14 January there was every indication that the British were poised to assault and so once more Rommel gave the order for his mechanized forces to begin pulling out. When 51st (Highland) Division began its attack on the night of 15 January, it faced nothing more than a deep minefield. Panzerarmee Afrika had gone. In the desert, the New Zealand and 7th Armoured Division found the going difficult. They were always poised to threaten the enemy, but each time were thwarted by his ability to slip away.

The Axis withdrawal was a staged affair. Its forces retreated in bounds of around 80km then stopped until there were signs that the British were close to outflanking them whereupon they would retreat again. Monty urged 51st Division to attack by night and day in order to catch the enemy. The main road was, as usual, left mined and cratered and the area to the south was difficult terrain, so the pursuit by Eighth Army was a slow one. Rommel eventually fell back on the Homs Line, the last defensive position before Tripoli, but had no intention of remaining there for long. On 20 January news reached him that British armour was in the hills to the south of him and captured orders showed that its objective was a point some 48km beyond Tripoli. Rommel decided he could delay no longer and gave the order for port demolitions to be increased and for Tripoli to be given up. There was no longer any tactical reason to hold the port for Axis ships could no longer reach it. Tripoli might be politically important for the Italians, but to Rommel its possession now counted for little. His new objective was a complete retreat from Tripolitania into Tunisia. After almost two years' campaigning, the Desert Fox was abandoning Libya and his superiors in Rome were most unhappy about it.

THE MARETH LINE

To everyone's surprise the British, on their drive through the mountains south of Tripoli, found the going very hard on the difficult terrain. The advance along the main road was also slowed almost to a standstill by fuel shortages, enemy demolitions and by the brave rearguard actions put up by 90. leichte-Division. The Afrika Korps was also busy opposing outflanking movements through the desert. As a consequence, the British did not reach Tripoli until 23 January. They found the port, as expected, severely damaged. The entrance to the harbour had been blocked by sunken ships and its approaches heavily mined. Port installations had been destroyed and their ruins booby-trapped. It took time to clear this damage and it was not until 2 February that the first supply ship entered the harbour.

To some it appeared that Rommel's decision to abandon Tripoli was a little premature. Rommel had been told that his withdrawal into Tunisia should be delayed as long as possible to allow for the completion of new

The Commonwealth War Graves Commission's cemetery at Sfax in Tunisia where many of those from Eighth Army who were killed at Mareth are buried. (WDBT-1, Steve Hamilton, Western Desert Battlefield Tours)

The strongpoint of Ksiba Est, the last bunker on the Mareth Line before the sea. (WDBT-7, Steve Hamilton, Western Desert Battlefield Tours)

defence works. The rapidity with which Rommel fell back shocked those in Rome. Kesselring and the Italians were furious with what they saw as a loss of nerve, protesting that Tripoli could have been held for much longer and the British advance delayed even more. Exasperated with the field marshal, they began briefing Hitler that it was time for Rommel to go and set in train discussions to choose his successor from the ranks of the Italian army.

The capture of Tripoli was a great triumph for Gen. Montgomery. On taking command of Eighth Army in August the previous year, his orders were to remove the enemy from Egypt, Cyrenaica and Tripolitania; this he had now done. Tripoli was the capital of Italian Libya and the goal of British troops ever since the conflict in North Africa had begun back in 1940. The capture of Tripoli demonstrated that the task was now almost complete and to celebrate this event a parade was held through the streets of the city in January attended by Prime Minister Churchill himself.

THE POSITION AT MARETH

Once Rommel had withdrawn his forces into Tunisia behind the Mareth Line, Axis occupation of the country could be divided into two mutually supporting fronts. Arnim's 5. Panzerarmee (PzAOK 5) would operate north of the area of Gabes, while Rommel faced southwards with his forces towards Eighth Army. On 24 January 1943, Kesselring told Arnim that he would be responsible for protecting the Mareth–Gabes area in Rommel's rear from any moves that the Americans might make towards the coast. Arnim's main objective was to continue aggressive action in the south-west to keep the Allies occupied. To this end, he was to assemble a mobile force capable of operating either against Allied First Army or any attack to the rear of the Mareth Line. Arnim had already been given 21. Panzer-Division from Panzerarmee Afrika, now called German–Italian First Army, to add to the 10. Panzer-Division he had under command. He also had the Italian Divisione Corrazzata 'Centauro' available, although all of its small numbers of tanks were at that time completely outdated.

The objectives of First Army in the rest of Tunisia mirrored those given to Arnim. It was also ordered to act aggressively to prevent Italian–German reinforcement of the Mareth Line to the detriment of Eighth Army. The campaign in north and south-west Tunisia between PzAOK 5 and First Army was to be the sideshow to the main event. Montgomery's attack at Mareth and its projected move along the coast towards Tunis was seen as the key Allied thrust. It was the success or failure of this advance that would eventually decide the fate of Axis forces in North Africa.

The Mareth Line consisted of a series of fortifications built by the French in the late 1930s to prevent any incursions into Tunisia from Italian-occupied Libya. It ran roughly from east to west in the area between Medenine and Gabes to guard the 36km-wide plain between the Matmata Hills and the sea. To the west of the hills was a stretch of desert known as the Dahar. The terrain here was largely broken desert and a series of salt marshes known as Chotts. At the northern end of the Dahar was a particularly large and seemingly impassable salt flat known as Chott Djerid. Farther to the east was an impenetrable area of soft sandy desert. This inhospitable ground behind the Matmata Hills stretched all the way into Algeria and made the coast route the only practical way into Tunisia from the south.

At the centre of the Mareth Line was the Wadi Zigzaou. This ran deep and wide across the plain and was lined with steep banks, in places over 20 metres high, with water flowing through itc centre forming a natural obstacle to motorized traffic. Wadi Zigzaou was the line's main position and it was along this natural feature that the French placed most of their concrete defences. Five kilometres in front of this deep anti-tank obstacle was another run-off from the hills which led down to the sea, the Wadi Zeuss. The area between the two wadis was sown with mines, both anti-tank and anti-personnel, and covered with wire. Mutually supporting weapons pits and deep trenches strengthened these defences.

The main coast road dissected the defence line into two halves, with the north-eastern part along the flat coastal plain being the most heavily defended. The line from the sea and up into the Matmata Hills was fortified with 26 strongpoints. In 1940, after France had capitulated to Germany and came under the control of the pro-Axis Vichy regime, the line was mostly demilitarized. There was no longer deemed to be a threat from Fascist-controlled Libya.

Rommel had long chosen the Mareth Line as his fallback position from which to face British Eighth Army. It was recognized as being the strongest defensive line in Africa, but its reputation did not impress the German commander. Although he accepted that its natural features and the Wadi Zigzaou combined into a formidable position, he saw much of the line as a collection of outdated French concrete blockhouses sited for an earlier kind of warfare. Many of the anti-tank emplacements were too small to hold German weapons and the line did not have sufficient depth to slow down the attacker other than during the initial stages. He was also worried that Montgomery might try something unorthodox to get behind the line. Early in February Rommel came to the conclusion that the Mareth Line did not live up to its reputation and that a far better defensive position was available 32km to the north at Wadi Akarit. Once again, Rommel was contemplating further withdrawals.

The Mareth Line completely blocked Montgomery's advance northwards along the coast road. The French had sited its defences to prevent such an advance. However, as military engineers have found throughout history, with every fixed line of defence there is always some method available for it to be overcome or outflanked, either by brute force or by skilful manoeuvre. Certainly Eighth Army had the brute force available to achieve the reduction of the line, provided its forces were applied with unrelenting pressure, but there was a more subtle option to consider by perhaps outflanking it.

The western anchor of the Mareth position was the Matmata Hills. The hills ran approximately north to south, parallel to the sea. Beyond the hills to the west was the Dahar. When the French built the line they were confident that movement through this broken ground by an attacking force was impracticable. Likewise an advance through the hills themselves by a large number of wheeled vehicles would be equally difficult with the transport then available. Those assumptions were made a decade before Eighth Army arrived in the area. There was a route through the hills and in 1943 there were four-wheel drive vehicles and tanks available to the British that could possibly make the journey. It would be difficult, it would be hazardous and it would hardly be possible to do it in secret, but it could be done.

Such an outflanking movement would get behind the Mareth defences, but would bring the attackers face to face with another problem. At the northern edge of the Matmata Hills was the Djebel Tebaga. Any advance by this route would then have to swing eastwards to get to the rear of the Mareth defences and the coast road at Gabes. Unfortunately, to do so would mean passing through the narrow gap between the Matmata Hills and Djebel Tebaga which was bound to be heavily defended.

In the short period available before the British arrived on the Mareth Line, many new field defences were established in front of Wadi Zigzaou. Two substantial new minefields were sown, both around 6km wide, irregularly shaped but running roughly parallel to the wadi. Barbed-wired barriers were established and well-sited anti-tank pits were dug, along with some new anti-tank ditches at vulnerable points. These new works formed the advance positions of the Mareth Line and were sited in order to be covered by artillery positions in the hills, but these positions themselves were vulnerable to being overlooked from high ground farther to the south. All of this new work was hastily assembled around the existing defences, but did little to overcome the flaws already identified by Rommel.

The question of Rommel's failing health and the Italian opposition to his continued presence at the head of Panzerarmee Afrika finally led to the decision to replace him. Hitler reluctantly agreed with Rome that the field marshal should return to Germany on sick leave in order to restore his health. He was to be replaced by Generale di Armata Giovanni Messe, veteran of the Eastern Front and a well-respected Italian commander, although the actual date for the changeover was left for Rommel to decide. As soon as this happened, Panzerarmee Afrika would become Italian First Army (AOK 1) and Arnim would take over all Axis forces in Tunisia at the head of a new

Men from the Maori battalion performing the *haka*, their traditional ancestral war cry. There is no doubting the strength and prowess of these warriors as they demonstrate their willingness to face their enemy in battle. (DA-01229 War History Collection, Alexander Turnbull Library, Wellington NZ)

command, Heeresgruppe Afrika. PzAOK 5 would then be commanded by Gen.Lt. Gustav von Vaerst. Overall command of the theatre would still reside with the Commando Supremo in Rome. By then Rommel was resigned to the changes and was ambivalent about the need for his replacement when told, remarking that Messe could take over as soon as he wanted to. He later commented: 'I had little desire to go on any longer playing the scapegoat for a pack of incompetents'.

Whilst Rommel was strengthening his positions at Mareth, Arnim's forces were keeping the Americans occupied. On 3 February, 21. Panzer-Division, now part of PzAOK 5, captured the pass at Faid from a small French contingent. The significance of this event was not lost on Rommel for he realized that the way was now open for an attack on the American supply centre at Gafsa. He knew that the Eighth Army would not be ready to attack Mareth for several more weeks and he could therefore spare some of his mobile forces for a dramatic venture. If Arnim agreed to attack towards Sidi Bou Zid with 10. Panzer-Division in conjunction with Rommel's proposed moves, then the Americans could be forced back into an awkward situation.

Kesselring was excited by this project when it was put to him and argued that the two commanders should go all out for the total destruction of the Americans. It was a bold proposal, although he was fearful that Rommel's health and resilience might not be up to the demands placed upon him. Kesselring was also aware that Arnim was waiting for Rommel's departure so that he might assume command of the whole of Heeresgruppe Afrika. Kesselring asked Arnim to be patient: 'let's give Rommel this one chance of glory before he gets out of Africa', he suggested.

The attack towards Sidi Bou Zid was launched by Arnim's deputy, Gen.Lt. Ziegler, on 12 February and surprised the Americans with its ferocity; by the end of the day they were in full retreat, which soon degenerated into a rout. On 17 February Rommel attacked towards Gafsa, but found that the Americans there had taken fright and pulled out. Over the next few days the advancing Panzer forces spread panic amongst the Americans who retreated in complete disorder, abandoning much of their equipment and leaving great numbers of their dead on the battlefield. For a while it looked as though the front would collapse as Rommel's force pushed through the pass at Kasserine and threatened the whole Allied lodgement in Tunisia. However, the Axis advance gradually slowed down through inaction by Arnim and because of a general lack of supplies. In the meantime British and French troops rallied to help the Americans stabilize their rear positions. By then Rommel had realized that he had overextended himself and placed his supply lines under too much pressure. Satisfied he had given the Americans a bloody nose, he withdrew his force back to the Mareth positions, leaving behind very chastised and worried American forces. (See Campaign 152: *Kasserine Pass 1943* for a full description of the Axis operation.)

A modern view of the anti-tank ditch built in front of the Wadi Zigzaou. (WDBT-6, Steve Hamilton, Western Desert Battlefield Tours)

Whilst Rommel and Arnim's venture in south-west Tunisia was running its course, Montgomery's army was moving inexorably forwards towards the Mareth Line. Advance units of Eighth Army were already in the area, but the great tail that stretched back to supply bases in Libya was taking time to close up. It would still be weeks before Monty was ready to do battle at Mareth. During Rommel's attacks towards Kasserine, the Americans had asked for Eighth Army to speed up these preparations so that it could initiate some sort of spoiling attack at Mareth to threaten Rommel's rear. Some agreement was reached, but before Montgomery could implement the moves the Desert Fox had pulled back into his defensive line.

Rommel's bold showing at Kasserine impressed Kesselring who thought that the venture demonstrated some of the field marshal's old spirit. At the end of the battle Kesselring made a bold decision. Even though it had been agreed with the Italians that Rommel would leave Tunisia on 22 February, Kesselring now suggested that Rommel, and not Arnim, should take command of Heeresgruppe Afrika. Messe would still control Italian First Army (AOK 1) and the German forces in the Mareth Line, but Rommel would have overall command of all Axis forces in the country. Needless to say, those in Rome were not pleased by the appointment, nor was Arnim, but the decision was ratified by Berlin.

Rommel's new command proved to be a hollow one. He was given no staff with which to operate and soon found out that decisions made in Rome were passed directly to his army commanders bypassing him. Arnim failed to consult Rommel in advance on any operation that he planned and when he decided to launch an attack towards Beja, Operation *Blockhead*, Rommel knew nothing of the move until it was under way. Worse was to come concerning the Mareth position.

THE BATTLE OF MEDENINE

Rommel was an expert at springing surprises. Whilst he waited at Mareth, he had for some time been considering launching an attack on Eighth Army before Montgomery was ready to start his assault. He hoped to take the British by surprise and leave them in disarray, buying more time for decisive attacks elsewhere in Tunisia.

On 28 February, Rommel summoned his generals to an operations group to work out a plan for the attack. The new army group commander discussed with Messe, Gen.Lt. Zeigler (in temporary command of the Afrika Korps pending the imminent arrival of Gen.Lt. Hans Cramer) and the armoured division commanders, how an attack on Eighth Army might be launched. He explained that Montgomery's main concentration area was around Medenine and its important road junctions. The town was just 8km in front of the Mareth Line and Rommel suggested that this was to be the objective of a surprise attack.

Messe was in command of the formation that would make the attack, the Italian First Army, and it was left that he should propose the final plan. Rommel had suggested a pincer attack with 10. and 21. Panzer-Divisionen striking from the north and 15. Panzer- and 164. leichte-Divisionen attacking from the south from the area of the Matmata Hills. Messe thought that the northern arm of this assault coming from the coastal plain would prove to be risky, for this was the area in which Montgomery had placed most of his artillery. It was also pointed out to Rommel that German engineers had sown this area with thousands of mines in front of Eighth Army. Many of these were booby-trapped and would take a long time to clear. Blowing them up would just alert the British. Everyone at the meeting seemed to go against the field marshal, perhaps realizing that he was no longer the military genius he once was and was a commander surviving on borrowed time. The conference lasted for five hours during which time Rommel gradually gave way and eventually turned the whole matter over to Messe. He was tired with the bickering and was resolved to wash his hands of it.

Messe's plan, Operation *Capri*, called for all of the attacks to be made in the south. The 10. Panzer-Division, with 40 tanks and with elements of 164. leichte-Division under command would advance out of the Matmata Hills northwards directly on Medenine with a small covering force farther south to prevent British reinforcements interfering. At the same time, 21. Panzer-Division with 40 tanks would attack from the west towards the small hills at Tadjera just north of Medenine which were thought to be the key to the British defences. The 15. Panzer-Division with 62 tanks would strike from the west at a position along the main road between Medenine and the Mareth Line, known to be the main assembly area for the forthcoming British attack. At the same time Italian Divisione 'La Spezia' with elements of German 90. leichte-Division would attack along the axis of the road from Mareth on the left flank of 15. Panzer-Division. All of these attacks would be from the right flank of the Mareth defence line out of the Matmata Hills.

A cheerful-looking American tank crew newly arrived in Tunisia. The setback suffered by the inexperienced Americans at Kasserine when they came up against crack German troops, brought a more sober attitude to the fighting. (US National Archives)

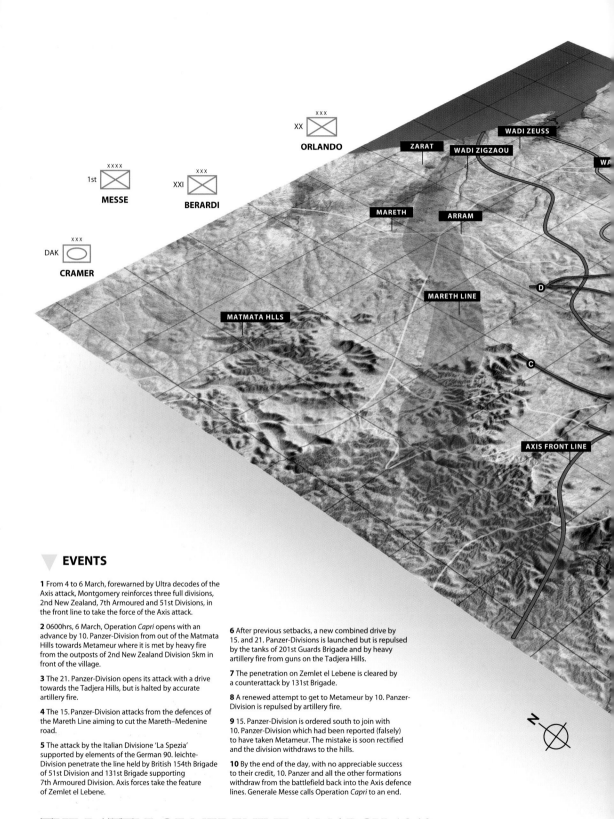

Map labels:
- ORLANDO (XX / XXX)
- MESSE 1st (XXXX)
- BERARDI XXI (XXX)
- CRAMER DAK (XXX)
- WADI ZEUSS
- ZARAT
- WADI ZIGZAOU
- MARETH
- ARRAM
- MARETH LINE
- MATMATA HLLS
- AXIS FRONT LINE
- D
- C

▼ EVENTS

1 From 4 to 6 March, forewarned by Ultra decodes of the Axis attack, Montgomery reinforces three full divisions, 2nd New Zealand, 7th Armoured and 51st Divisions, in the front line to take the force of the Axis attack.

2 0600hrs, 6 March, Operation *Capri* opens with an advance by 10. Panzer-Division from out of the Matmata Hills towards Metameur where it is met by heavy fire from the outposts of 2nd New Zealand Division 5km in front of the village.

3 The 21. Panzer-Division opens its attack with a drive towards the Tadjera Hills, but is halted by accurate artillery fire.

4 The 15. Panzer-Division attacks from the defences of the Mareth Line aiming to cut the Mareth–Medenine road.

5 The attack by the Italian Divisione 'La Spezia' supported by elements of the German 90. leichte-Division penetrate the line held by British 154th Brigade of 51st Division and 131st Brigade supporting 7th Armoured Division. Axis forces take the feature of Zemlet el Lebene.

6 After previous setbacks, a new combined drive by 15. and 21. Panzer-Divisions is launched but is repulsed by the tanks of 201st Guards Brigade and by heavy artillery fire from guns on the Tadjera Hills.

7 The penetration on Zemlet el Lebene is cleared by a counterattack by 131st Brigade.

8 A renewed attempt to get to Metameur by 10. Panzer-Division is repulsed by artillery fire.

9 15. Panzer-Division is ordered south to join with 10. Panzer-Division which had been reported (falsely) to have taken Metameur. The mistake is soon rectified and the division withdraws to the hills.

10 By the end of the day, with no appreciable success to their credit, 10. Panzer and all the other formations withdraw from the battlefield back into the Axis defence lines. Generale Messe calls Operation *Capri* to an end.

THE BATTLE OF MEDENINE, 6 MARCH 1943

The battle of Medenine, code name Operation *Capri*, was the last Axis attack in North Africa. It was aimed at disrupting Montgomery's preparations for Eighth Army's assault on the Mareth Line.

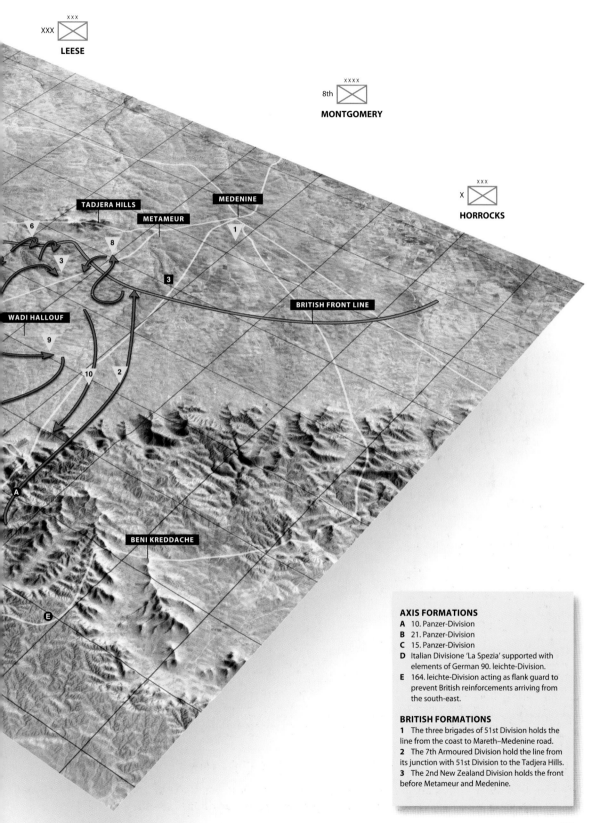

Note: Gridlines are shown at intervals of 5km/3.1miles

XXX XXX **LEESE**

8th XXXX **MONTGOMERY**

X XXX **HORROCKS**

TADJERA HILLS

METAMEUR

MEDENINE

6

8

3

3

WADI HALLOUF

9

10 2

BRITISH FRONT LINE

A

BENI KREDDACHE

E

AXIS FORMATIONS
A 10. Panzer-Division
B 21. Panzer-Division
C 15. Panzer-Division
D Italian Divisione 'La Spezia' supported with elements of German 90. leichte-Division.
E 164. leichte-Division acting as flank guard to prevent British reinforcements arriving from the south-east.

BRITISH FORMATIONS
1 The three brigades of 51st Division holds the line from the coast to Mareth–Medenine road.
2 The 7th Armoured Division hold the line from its junction with 51st Division to the Tadjera Hills.
3 The 2nd New Zealand Division holds the front before Metameur and Medenine.

53

In his memoirs Montgomery remarked that he thought Rommel would attack in a certain way and that he planned to deal with it on ground of his own choosing. In fact he was forewarned by Ultra intercepts and knew exactly what Italian First Army intended to do. He therefore moved 7th Armoured Division and infantry from 131st Brigade from the south into the area in front of Medenine which would take the brunt of the attack by 15. and 21. Panzer-Divisionen. He also reinforced the whole of his front so that he eventually had three full divisions in the line: 51st Infantry, 7th Armoured and 2nd New Zealand Divisions. Elements of 4th Indian Division and 201st Guards Armoured Brigade were placed in reserve.

British XXX Corps facing Messe had a veritable arsenal of weapons with which to deal with the attack: 350 25-pdr field and medium guns, 460 anti-tank guns and 300 tanks. Italian First Army had much less firepower available and sparse amounts of fuel and ammunition. It was able to put just 124 assorted field guns, 96 anti-tank guns and 142 tanks into the attack. Not only was the assault being made without any sort of superiority in any sector, their opponents knew exactly when they were coming and where they were aiming for.

Operation *Capri* opened on 6 March at 0630hrs when the Axis artillery opened fire through a thick morning mist. It immediately ran into trouble as the tanks began to move out into the open ground that led to their objectives. Lessons learned by Eighth Army at Alamein proved to be deadly. British artillery held its fire until its guns could be used at close range in concentrated barrages. Its objective was to destroy the enemy formations en masse and not to disperse them with harassing fire. Likewise the anti-tank guns were sited to

Generale Messe's attack at Medenine, instigated by Rommel, resulted in the already-dwindling numbers of German tanks and their crews being reduced even further with absolutely nothing gained. (IWM, NA1043)

Three knocked-out Panzers after the battle of Medenine. British tactics of using anti-tank guns en masse and holding fire until the enemy tanks had advanced close enough for every shot to count, rather than firing too early and dispersing the enemy, was a resounding success. (IWM, NA1042)

kill enemy tanks, not to support their own, and they allowed the Panzers to approach close enough for every shot to count, rather than opening fire too soon and causing the enemy's armour to scatter. One after another German tanks burst into flames or slewed out of line damaged. Machine guns firing on fixed lines dealt effectively with the supporting *Panzergrenadiers*.

Rommel tried to watch the battle from the high ground to the south, but for a long while could see little through the mist. When it finally cleared he could observe the futility of the assault. He could plainly see that Montgomery was aware of the attack and its objectives. The movement of the British armour from the south to the centre gave every indication of having been forewarned. He blamed his Italian allies for the lapse in security, believing some high officer had betrayed the operation. Messe urged attacks to go in again and again, each suffering the same result. By late afternoon Rommel had seen enough and told Messe to call off the attack. 'A pincer attack would have been much more successful,' he bitterly commented. The battle of Medenine had been costly to the Axis forces for they lost around 50 of their 142 tanks and took 635 casualties. In contrast, the British official history of the campaign called their losses 'trifling'.

Montgomery once again thought that he had got the better of Rommel, but it was not Rommel's battle. The Desert Fox had lost all power and influence and was resigned to the inevitability of the attack ending badly. He was also convinced that a complete defeat in North Africa was inevitable. Once again he cabled Rome with a request to withdraw from Mareth to a shorter position at Enfidaville where AOK 1 and PzAOK 5 could combine on a strong defensive line. When Hitler heard of the proposal he was again furious and quickly dismissed the idea, as did the Commando Supremo in Rome. Rommel had now made this defeatist request to withdraw once too often and no one in power believed in him any longer. He had completely lost his magic touch. Everyone knew that it was now time for Rommel to go.

Rommel heard of Hitler's angry rebuttal of his proposal at the end of the day of the Medenine attack. He suddenly felt too sick to carry on. The next day he took leave of his generals and waited for Arnim to come and see him. On 8 March he handed over Heeresgruppe Afrika and, early the next morning, 9 March, drove to Sfax and boarded an aircraft for Rome. He was never to set foot in North Africa again.

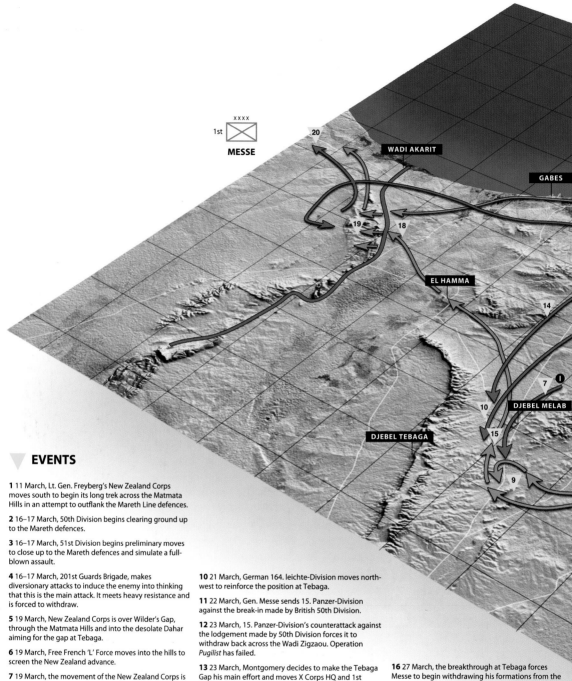

EVENTS

1 11 March, Lt. Gen. Freyberg's New Zealand Corps moves south to begin its long trek across the Matmata Hills in an attempt to outflank the Mareth Line defences.

2 16–17 March, 50th Division begins clearing ground up to the Mareth defences.

3 16–17 March, 51st Division begins preliminary moves to close up to the Mareth defences and simulate a full-blown assault.

4 16–17 March, 201st Guards Brigade, makes diversionary attacks to induce the enemy into thinking that this is the main attack. It meets heavy resistance and is forced to withdraw.

5 19 March, New Zealand Corps is over Wilder's Gap, through the Matmata Hills and into the desolate Dahar aiming for the gap at Tebaga.

6 19 March, Free French 'L' Force moves into the hills to screen the New Zealand advance.

7 19 March, the movement of the New Zealand Corps is detected and Gen. Mannerini concentrates his Saharan Group to block the Tebaga Gap.

8 20–21 March, Montgomery launches Operation *Pugilist* against the defences of the Mareth Line with 50th Division. The attack by just one brigade is initially successful, but is counterattacked over the following two days and nights and makes little progress inland.

9 21 March, Freyberg's New Zealand Corps arrives at the Tebaga Gap and begins to attack its defences, but is unable to break through.

10 21 March, German 164. leichte-Division moves north-west to reinforce the position at Tebaga.

11 22 March, Gen. Messe sends 15. Panzer-Division against the break-in made by British 50th Division.

12 23 March, 15. Panzer-Division's counterattack against the lodgement made by 50th Division forces it to withdraw back across the Wadi Zigzaou. Operation *Pugilist* has failed.

13 23 March, Montgomery decides to make the Tebaga Gap his main effort and moves X Corps HQ and 1st Armoured Division across the Matmata Hills to join the New Zealanders. Indian 4th Division simultaneously tries to make its way along the hills in the centre.

14 25 March, Messe detects the movement of X Corps towards the Tebaga Gap and orders 21. Panzer-Division to join 164. leichte-Division.

15 26 March, Lt. Gen. Horrocks launches Operation *Supercharge II* against the Tebaga Gap. By the next morning 1st Armoured Division is through and advancing on El Hamma.

16 27 March, the breakthrough at Tebaga forces Messe to begin withdrawing his formations from the Mareth Line into a new line at Wadi Akarit.

17 29 March, XXX Corps follows up the retreating Axis forces towards the Wadi Akarit position.

18 30 March, Eighth Army reach the defences of the Wadi Akarit Line.

19 6 April British XXX Corps attacks Axis forces holding the line at Wadi Akarit.

20 7 April, XXX Corps breaks through the Wadi Akarit Line and continues to pursue Messe's army northwards.

OPERATIONS AGAINST THE MARETH LINE

The failure of Montgomery's direct attack on the Mareth defences forced him to switch his main effort to an outflanking movement to get behind the Axis position.

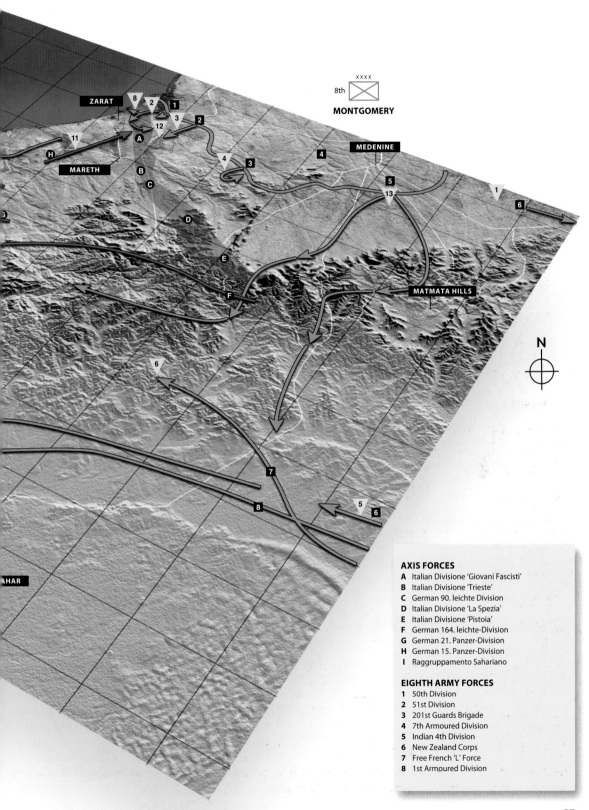

Note: Gridlines are shown at intervals of 10km/6.21miles

ZARAT

8 2 1
3
12 2
11
A
H
MARETH
B
C
D
E
F
4
3
4
MEDENINE
5
13
1
6

8th
xxxx
MONTGOMERY

MATMATA HILLS

6

7

8 5 6

N

AXIS FORCES
A   Italian Divisione 'Giovani Fascisti'
B   Italian Divisione 'Trieste'
C   German 90. leichte Division
D   Italian Divisione 'La Spezia'
E   Italian Divisione 'Pistoia'
F   German 164. leichte-Division
G   German 21. Panzer-Division
H   German 15. Panzer-Division
I   Raggruppamento Sahariano

EIGHTH ARMY FORCES
1   50th Division
2   51st Division
3   201st Guards Brigade
4   7th Armoured Division
5   Indian 4th Division
6   New Zealand Corps
7   Free French 'L' Force
8   1st Armoured Division

Rommel's departure from Tunisia was kept secret from the public. The Allies had no idea that he had left the theatre for almost two months, believing that in the final battles for Tunis he was still at the head of Axis forces. Rommel travelled to Rome and Berlin and forcefully gave his views on the situation in Tunisia and the hopelessness of carrying on fighting. He pointed out that unless the forces there were quickly evacuated, they would be lost. No one was listening to him. The war in Africa was forced to rumble on to its inevitable conclusion, just as he had predicted.

ASSAULTING THE MARETH LINE

On 28 February, Commander Allied 18th Army Group, Gen. Alexander, issued his intentions for the coming months. The prime objective was to destroy the entire enemy force in Tunisia. This would be done in two phases. First, Eighth Army would pass through the Mareth Line and advance through the Gabes Gap between Gabes and Wadi Akarit. It would be helped during this phase by First Army which would mount controlled attacks to secure dominating areas and to prevent enemy forces being moved against it. The second phase would involve both armies attacking towards Tunis to close a net around Axis forces which would lead to their complete destruction. These moves would be made to a tight timescale, for the campaign in Tunisia had to be finished by 30 April in order for the proposed invasion of Sicily to be launched before August.

Messe's attack at Medenine had caused Montgomery little concern. Forewarned and prepared for the onslaught, Eighth Army took it in its stride and suffered only minimal interference with its preparations for the Mareth attack. As things settled down, Monty formulated his final plan. He had for some time been considering how he would breach the Mareth Line. He knew that the main attack against the defences would have to be head on, barging its way forwards along or near the axis of the highway that ran through Medenine towards Gabes. He also considered how he might launch an outflanking operation in conjunction with this attack through the Tebaga Gap to the north to get behind the Mareth position. This move would threaten Messe's rear and cause some of the Axis' strength in the line to be drawn away. To do this he would have to put a large force either through the Matmata Hills or along the edge of the broken ground of the Dahar.

Before he could commit to this outflanking movement, Montgomery had to discover a practicable route across what was very inhospitable ground. To make the move a serious threat at least an infantry division together with supporting armour would have to make the passage. The first problem was to find a way into the Dahar at a point well clear of the Mareth Line. This task was given to a patrol from the Long Range Desert Group under the command of Captain Wilder.

In early January whilst Eighth Army was still in Libya, Wilder made a reconnaissance patrol into the Matmata Hills. At a point some 48km south-west of Foum Tatahouine he found a pass that led through into the Dahar, which, understandably, was labelled 'Wilder's Gap'. A later patrol led by Lt. Tinker went through the pass and penetrated along the Dahar as far as Djebel Tebaga and examined the Tebaga Gap, verifying that the route would be suitable to carry the outflanking force that Montgomery envisaged.

With the confirmation that he was looking for, Montgomery could formulate a plan for tackling the Mareth Line. He decided that he would give the task of making the outflanking movement to Lt. Gen. Freyberg and his 2nd New Zealand Division. The formation would be strengthened for the attack by the addition of 8th Armoured Brigade and a regiment of armoured cars from 1st King's Dragoon Guards. For extra firepower regiments of medium artillery, anti-tank guns and light anti-aircraft guns were added to Freyberg's command. Leclerc's 'L' Force and the Free French Flying Column

Two New Zealand members of the Long Range Desert Group. The unit's ability to traverse the wide open spaces of desert undetected enabled them to carry out covert reconnaissance patrols and intelligence missions behind enemy lines. Many of the original members of the group were New Zealand volunteers. (DA-00064, War History Collection, Alexander Turnbull Library, Wellington NZ)

were also to form part of the group. This enlargement resulted in the formation being designated the New Zealand Corps, although no extra administrative staff were added and Freyberg was expected to command both the division and the corps.

Freyberg's corps was to make the complicated manoeuvre over the Matmata Hills and through the Dahar, undetected as much as possible, to be in contact with the enemy at Tebaga on the night of the main attack against the Mareth Line, 20–21 March. This would involve a movement of over 400km. 'L' Force would hold the area of Ksar Rhilane on the edge of the salt marshes to protect the corps' left flank during the advance and then move onto the Matmata Hills during the attack phase. The moves were to start from the Medenine area on 11 March.

Meanwhile Gen. Messe continued preparations to cope with the British assault. To man the line he used Italian formations interspaced with German units. On the coastal plain from north-east to south-west was the Italian XX Corpo with 136ᵃ ('Giovani Fascisti' – Young Fascists) and 101ᵃ ('Trieste') Divisioni. The German Luftwaffe 19. Flak-Division reinforced this zone with 16 dual-purpose 88mm Flak batteries and numerous 20mm anti-aircraft batteries. In the centre German 90. leichte-Division held the sector across the main highway to Gabes. The western portion of the line was held by Italian XXI Corpo consisting of 80ᵃ ('La Spezia') and 16ᵃ ('Pistoia') Divisioni. On the extreme western end of the line, the German 164. leichte-Division covered the ground spreading up into the Matmata Hills holding the road through the Hallouf Pass which led up to the village of Matmata.

Holding the north-west rear of the Mareth positions towards the Tebaga Gap was the Raggruppamento Sahariano (Italian Saharan Group), a collection of around nine battalions of infantry and 11 batteries of guns. Messe's reserve, placed to the rear of the line, consisted of the 1st Luftwaffe Brigade near the coast behind the Giovani Fascisti, Panzergrenadier Regiment Afrika covering the Gabes road and 15. Panzer-Division on the western side of the defensive positions. Farther to the rear was 21. Panzer-Division in a position from which it was able to move either

Operation *Pugilist*: the main attack on the Mareth defences

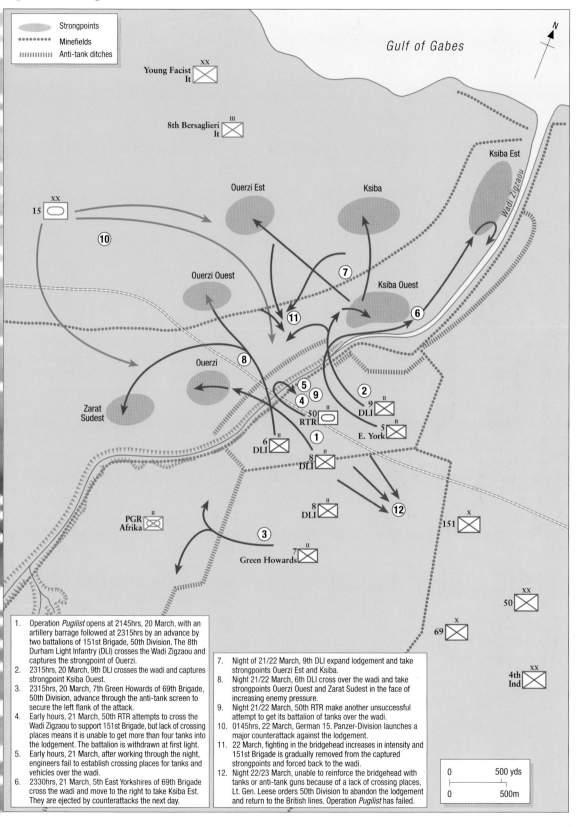

Legend:
- Strongpoints
- Minefields
- Anti-tank ditches

Gulf of Gabes

N

Young Facist
It — XX

8th Bersaglieri
It — III

Ksiba Est

15 — XX

(10)

Ouerzi Est

Ksiba

Wadi Zigzaou

Ouerzi Ouest

(7)

Ksiba Ouest

(11)

(6)

(8)

Ouerzi

(5) (9)

(4) (9)

2
9 DLI — II

Zarat
Sudest

50
RTR

(1)

5 E. York — II

6 DLI — II

8 DLI — II

PGR
Afrika — II

8 DLI — II

(12)

151 — X

(3)

Green Howards — II

50 — XX

69 — X

4th Ind — XX

1. Operation *Pugilist* opens at 2145hrs, 20 March, with an artillery barrage followed at 2315hrs by an advance by two battalions of 151st Brigade, 50th Division. The 8th Durham Light Infantry (DLI) crosses the Wadi Zigzaou and captures the strongpoint of Ouerzi.
2. 2315hrs, 20 March, 9th DLI crosses the wadi and captures strongpoint Ksiba Ouest.
3. 2315hrs, 20 March, 7th Green Howards of 69th Brigade, 50th Division, advance through the anti-tank screen to secure the left flank of the attack.
4. Early hours, 21 March, 50th RTR attempts to cross the Wadi Zigzaou to support 151st Brigade, but lack of crossing places means it is unable to get more than four tanks into the lodgement. The battalion is withdrawn at first light.
5. Early hours, 21 March, after working through the night, engineers fail to establish crossing places for tanks and vehicles over the wadi.
6. 2330hrs, 21 March, 5th East Yorkshires of 69th Brigade cross the wadi and move to the right to take Ksiba Est. They are ejected by counterattacks the next day.

7. Night of 21/22 March, 9th DLI expand lodgement and take strongpoints Ouerzi Est and Ksiba.
8. Night 21/22 March, 6th DLI cross over the wadi and take strongpoints Ouerzi Ouest and Zarat Sudest in the face of increasing enemy pressure.
9. Night 21/22 March, 50th RTR make another unsuccessful attempt to get its battalion of tanks over the wadi.
10. 0145hrs, 22 March, German 15. Panzer-Division launches a major counterattack against the lodgement.
11. 22 March, fighting in the bridgehead increases in intensity and 151st Brigade is gradually removed from the captured strongpoints and forced back to the wadi.
12. Night 22/23 March, unable to reinforce the bridgehead with tanks or anti-tank guns because of a lack of crossing places, Lt. Gen. Leese orders 50th Division to abandon the lodgement and return to the British lines. Operation *Pugilist* has failed.

0   500 yds
0   500m

General Leclerc, commander of Free French Force 'L', jokes with some British tankers after the battle. (US National Archives)

north against the Americans or south against Eighth Army as the situation dictated. The 10. Panzer-Division was located much farther north beyond Gabes ready to be called into action if required.

All these formations were well below their nominal strength in men, tanks and guns. Estimates suggested that Italian First Army had 50,000 German troops and around 35,000 Italians, with approximately 440 guns and 140 tanks. This was well below what Eighth Army could put into the field. Although it was on a par with Axis forces regarding infantry, both having around 43 infantry battalions, Eighth Army was superior in tanks with 743 runners and had 692 guns available.

For the main assault on the Mareth Line, Montgomery proposed to use both of his other corps. His administration and supply set-up was at such a high level that he could now confidently put two corps into the line. As was his nature, he refused to move before he was completely ready. Once again there was pressure from London to mount the attack sooner, but Montgomery resisted this interference until he felt that he had enough supplies to maintain these two corps right through until the end of the campaign in Tunisia.

XXX Corps was to lead the attack on the Mareth Line near the coast at the same time as the New Zealand Corps' attack. It would then swing westwards to roll up the enemy positions from east to west. X Corps would then pass through and exploit towards Gabes. The simultaneous assaults by the two corps would force Messe to split his armour to deal with them. The most sensitive area for AOK 1's commander would be that at Tebaga, for, if Freyberg broke through there, he would be behind the Mareth Line and commanding the coastal road. This would make him capable of sealing off all Axis forces to the south. If Messe did not move quickly enough his whole army would be caught in a trap. Montgomery planned for just such an event. He intended that once the line had been broken into, X Corps would make a swift advance northwards pressing the enemy hard to prevent him making a further stand at Wadi Akarit. Montgomery's orders, given in the final plan of attack, Operation *Pugilist*, published on 26 February were precise: 'Once operations have begun on the night of 20–21 March they will be conducted relentlessly until Sfax has been reached.'

THE BREAK-IN ATTACK

After the Axis attack on Medenine, Eighth Army adjusted its hold on the line in preparation for the main assault on the Mareth position. XXX Corps held the forward area with 50th Division on the right near the coast, 51st Division in the centre and 7th Armoured Division holding the area astride the Medenine–Gabes road. They all faced the enemy just short of his defensive outposts in front of Wadi Zeuss. Farther south 4th Indian Division had arrived and was positioned just back from the front. Before the set-piece battle could open, the attacking division needed to close on the enemy's main defence line.

Lieutenant-General Leese had decided to make his initial assault with Maj. Gen. Nichols' 50th Division. The 51st Division would then exploit the breakthrough and help clear the line opening a gap through which 7th Armoured

Troops of 50th Division clearing one of the trenches amongst the strongpoints of the Mareth defence line. The picture was most likely taken after the event, rather than in the heat of battle. (IWM, NA1336)

SHERMAN TANKS FROM 8TH ARMOURED BRIGADE ADVANCE THROUGH WILDER'S GAP DURING THE NEW ZEALAND CORPS' OPERATION TO OUTFLANK THE MARETH LINE (pp. 64–65)

The route through Wilder's Gap enabled Lt. Gen. Freyberg VC to get over the Matmata Hills (1) into the area of desert between Tunisia and Algeria known as the Dahar. This advance through broken and desolate terrain was along a single dusty track previously only used by Bedouins. It had been scouted as a possible route through the hills just weeks before. Along this single track, Freyberg negotiated the whole of his command in secret, hoping to spring a surprise on Gen. Messe's rear and outflank the defences of the Mareth Line.

Lieutenant-General Sir Bernard Freyberg VC (2), commanding the New Zealand 2nd Division, was a highly decorated veteran of World War I. His command was unusual in that he had the power of veto over tasks assigned to the formation. If ordered to commit to an assignment that he was not happy with, he would insist that he had to refer the decision back to his masters in New Zealand. This gave him considerable control over the way his division was employed which often exasperated other commanders. Freyberg was none the less an extremely accomplished tactician and had shown his powers of manoeuvre through a number of skilful executed left hooks to outflank German positions during the advance to Tripoli.

Freyberg was always to be seen up with the leading troops close to the action. He had been wounded nine times during the Great War and was to be injured twice more during World War II. Churchill called him 'the salamander', a reference to the mythical belief of that creature's love of fire. Freyberg had the personal use of a Stuart tank (3), fitted with a wooden dummy gun and a host of communications equipment. This was his command vehicle in action and he was often seen standing on its roof urging troops along. Close by in the commander's Ford station wagon (4), his long-suffering staff tried to keep up with their energetic general.

The reinforcement of Freyberg's division to corps status involved the addition of an armoured brigade. The 8th Armoured Brigade, which was assigned to the division, comprised 3rd Royal Tank Regiment together with the Nottinghamshire and Staffordshire Yeomanries. It was one of the best available to Eighth Army. The brigade had gradually been updating its tanks since Alamein, replacing its unreliable British Crusaders with American Shermans (5).

Division would pass to deal with the expected Panzer counterattack. It would launch this main advance on the night of 20–21 March against the sector of the line near the coast between the two strongpoints of Ouerzi and Ksiba Ouest.

First the 50th Division had to clear the minefields and outposts in front of Wadi Zeuss. Starting on 16–17 March, it would then cross the deep channel and finally settle itself before the much larger and more heavily defended Wadi Zigzaou, ready for the main operation four days later. Such a move would, however, alert the enemy to that sector of the line and prepare him for the main blow when it fell. To help divert this unwanted attention, two other diversionary attacks were to take place simultaneously with that of 50th Division.

On the night of 16–17 March, these preliminary moves began. The 50th Division started attacking the area in front of it, eliminating the enemy outposts and marking routes through the minefields as planned. At the same time 51st Division on its left was also on the move, clearing its way forwards over the Wadi Zeuss, whilst farther south 201st Guards Brigade attacked an area of higher ground between the two wadis. The strength and diversity of these moves were designed to leave the Axis defenders unable to determine where the main blow would fall. It was hoped the attack by the Guards Brigade with tanks in the centre would imply that this was the precursor to the main assault.

The 50th and 51st Divisions took their objectives without too much opposition, each skilfully edging their way forwards against Italian defenders

Troops of 51st Division inspect one of the Mareth bunkers. (IWM, NA1536)

Modern view of one of the bunkers of the Ouerzi strongpoint on the Mareth Line overlooking Wadi Zigzaou. (WDBT-5, Steve Hamilton, Western Desert Battlefield Tours)

supported by the combined guns of both divisions. The Guards Brigade was less successful; it had the misfortune to meet unsuspected minefields and opposition from German 90. leichte-Division. The Guards battalions managed to reach their objectives through the strong enemy resistance, but were unable to get supporting weapons forwards. Heavy shelling and mortar fire thwarted any open movement throughout the next day. Unable to progress farther towards the main enemy line, it was decided that, as this particular diversion had failed, the brigade should withdraw.

The opening moves by Eighth Army concentrated enemy minds on the forthcoming attack. However, on 19 March, the day before Operation *Pugilist* was to be launched, Montgomery learned via Ultra decrypts that Freyberg's corps had been spotted. By then the New Zealand Corps was well on its way through the Dahar closing on the area of the Tebaga Gap. Hopes of a surprise attack through the gap towards El Hamma were now lost. Eighth Army's commander signalled Freyberg to press on regardless of security and launch his attack as soon as he arrived at his objective. The loss of surprise was a blow, but some good could still come of it. Generale Messe now knew that his Mareth position was about to be attacked from both the front and the rear. It now required some good generalship on his part to decide how he would use his reserves to deal with the startling news.

Lieutenant-General Freyberg's corps had begun its long trek on 11 March from a position close to Medenine where it had been helping to deal with the enemy attack five days earlier. The constituent parts of the corps were gradually assembled and provided with 11 days' rations, water and ammunition together with fuel for 560km. It headed south through Foum Tatahouine, moving away from the Mareth Line for some 105km, before swinging westwards towards

Wilder's Gap. Just before the convoys began slowly grinding their way up through the Matmata Hills, the tanks of 8th Armoured Brigade were unloaded from the tank transporters that had brought them forwards. From here onwards, all tracked vehicles were under their own power for the long slog over the hills and through the Dahar towards the Tebaga Gap.

Over the next seven days the vehicles of the New Zealand Corps threaded through the mountains, along a single narrow road across difficult terrain, to reach an assembly area on the edge of the Dahar. When all was ready, on 19 March, the corps moved on to the staging area close to Ksar Rhilane and Gen. Leclerc's 'L' Force. The French units in this area had recently seen action against a small German armoured scouting force, but determined resistance by the Free French and some help from the RAF repulsed the attack. The clash did, however, serve warning to Messe that the Eighth Army was up to something in the western desert.

'We moved all night on March 19th,' Freyberg later reported, 'intending to make a surprise march by night on 20th to coincide with a frontal assault on the Mareth Line. When however it seemed likely that the enemy was aware of our assembly we decided to waste no further effort on deception but to rely entirely on speed. We therefore moved in daylight on 20th in desert formation and raced north to break through to El Hamma and Gabes.' The going through the desert was never good and it gradually got worse when the advance units of the corps hit more of the salt flats. Progress by night became difficult and it was not until the afternoon of the 21st that Freyberg's armoured cars made contact with the enemy in the Tebaga Gap.

A Valentine tank of 50th RTR immobilized in the soggy bottom of the Wadi Zigzaou. The remains of piles of wooden fascines which were supposed to give traction through the water and up the banks of the wadi can be seen churned up in the rear. The attack by 50th RTR was completely upset by this most difficult of natural barriers. (IWM, NA1348)

This interesting picture shows just how much rock had to be blown out to provide safe access to this bunker via trenches. It overlooks a road or track through some steep terrain and may well have been located up in the Matmata Hills rather than near the coast. (IWM, E22843)

The main attack on the Mareth Line began on the night of 20–21 March. A terrific bombardment, the largest since Alamein, opened the assault in the coastal sector held by 50th Division. Additional fire was laid down by three medium and three field regiments on the village of Arram on the Medenine–Gabes road to act as a diversion. The size of the opening barrage signalled the start of what should have been a massive assault on the Mareth Line, but the numbers of troops going into the attack were rather low. Even though Montgomery had two full corps to hand, only two battalions of infantry were initially used to assault the enemy defences on a very narrow front.

Historians have for decades puzzled over why Monty attacked with so few men, supported by just one regiment of outdated and outgunned Valentine tanks, in such a relatively tight area. Certainly at that time Eighth Army's commander felt on top form having just days before fought a successful defensive action at Medenine. He had brought his army almost 3,200km across North Africa without a single major setback and was no doubt feeling in total command of the situation. He had great confidence in his own army and his own tactical genius and viewed the enemy, especially the Italian defenders at Mareth, as being less capable. In simple terms he was overconfident approaching the battle and thought that he could bring about a victory with a simple break-in and a massive rapid exploitation. He was not expecting to have to grind out a victory.

The 50th Division's 151st Brigade was given the task of making the breakthrough. Its 9th Durham Light Infantry (DLI) was to capture the strongpoint of Ksiba Ouest, whilst 8th DLI tried to gain that at Ouerzi. In the centre, 50th Royal Tank Regiment (RTR) was to follow the two lead battalions, cross the Wadi Zigzaou and then fan out in the rear of the forward defences. The brigade's 6th DLI was to mop up and consolidate. Just before the attack, a battalion of infantry from 69th Brigade (7th Green Howards) would capture a knoll of high ground on the left flank in front of the wadi which overlooked the assault. To deal with the anti-tank nature of the Wadi Zigzaou a large number of fascines were assembled to be dropped into place to allow tanks and vehicles to cross. Climbing ladders were also provided for the infantry.

At 2315hrs, 90 minutes after the preliminary bombardment had opened, 50th Division's attack got under way. Counter-fire from the enemy was fierce as the two lead battalions made for their objectives. Two troops of Scorpion flail tanks cleared the anti-personnel mines in front of the wadi right up to the watercourse itself. The infantry then braved the machine guns aimed along the wadi and scrambled up the high banks on the far side. Mortar and artillery fire descended on the attacking troops as the two lead battalions made for their objectives. Small-arms fire from the strongpoints picked off a few of the leading men, but momentum carried the others forwards. The men of the Durham Light Infantry pressed through the wire into the trenches that zigzagged across defended localities and then close-quarter fighting, at the end of the bayonet, put the Italian defenders to flight. By the middle of the night both Ksiba Ouest and Ouerzi were taken.

Back in the wadi, the Valentine tanks of 50th RTR made for the crossing place opposite Ouerzi. Sappers blew a section of the high bank to create a slope up to the top of the deep watercourse and the tanks came forward to drop their fascines into the water to improve their traction across the mud. Unfortunately, their flailing tracks created even more mud and ground into the soft bottom of the wadi resulting in the leading tank sticking fast and blocking the crossing place. Other tanks tried to manoeuvre round the helpless Valentine but succeeded only in creating more chaos, halting the progress of the remainder of the regiment pressing behind them.

This churning mass of armour attracted heavy artillery fire on the crossing place causing serious casualties to the exposed engineers working in the wadi. Urged on by their commanders to get across, individual tanks struggled to find a way over. With the aid of brave engineers, four Valentines actually got up the far bank. As the night progressed, it soon became clear that few more tanks would get over before daylight, so it was decided to pull the rest of the regiment back to its assembly area.

Two other crossings of Wadi Zigzaou had been planned for that night, but both came to nothing when the engineers were forced to give up the task due to accurate enemy fire. At the end of the night the attack could be seen as a failure. Some small gains had been made, a few tanks were across, but no anti-tank guns were up with the two exposed battalions that had made the assault. Daylight brought increasingly accurate enemy fire along the whole of the wadi. The division's commander, Maj. Gen. Nichols, decided to hold fast and to try again the next night.

There was little improvement on 21 March. The exposed troops over the Wadi Zigzaou had to endure much heavy fighting, some of which was at very close quarters. The enemy had moved some troops of 90. leichte-Division eastwards to help the Italian Young Fascists deal with the assault. Few heavy weapons were brought over the wadi to improve the lot of 151st Brigade, although 6th DLI was deployed to clear strongpoints to the west of the lodgement. When darkness fell, 50th Division tried again, this time with the help of elements of 51st Highland Division who attempted to deal with the enemy fire that was most troublesome to the crossing places. Sappers had

Modern view of the battlefield of the Tebaga Gap with the remains of the Roman wall in the foreground. (WDBT-2, Steve Hamilton, Western Desert Battlefield Tours)

once again opened a route across the wadi and the remainder of 50th RTR's Valentine tanks were passed over. Their passage through the soft muddy bottom and up the ramped sides of the wadi totally destroyed the crossing place to the extent that, once again, no anti-tank guns could be brought across. Attempts to repair the damage were thwarted next morning when heavy rain showers deepened the water in the wadi and the exhausted engineers were forced to call off their attempts to open a new crossing place.

The continued perseverance with the small bridgehead near the coast by the British enabled Gen. Messe to feel confident enough to believe that the attack was a major one. He therefore committed part of his reserve and sent 15. Panzer-Division south to deal with the bridgehead on the 22nd. With the location of Eighth Army's attack in the east now known, Messe also decided he could thin out the other end of the Mareth defences in the west and so gave orders for 164. leichte-Division to move northwards to help stop the New Zealand Corps forcing its way through the Tebaga Gap.

That same day Montgomery ordered a renewed assault and a strengthening of the lodgement to go ahead after dark. Unfortunately, far from renewing the attack, Maj. Gen. Nichols' division was forced to defend its small gains when its exposed troops were hit by a vigorous counterattack by Panzers and *Panzergrenadiers*. Even some of Ramcke's paratroopers were thrown against them.

Very soon each of the captured strongpoints was retaken. The poorly gunned Valentine tanks could not deal with the more heavily armed PzKpfw IIIs and IVs and were picked off one by one. In the face of this great pressure the exposed battalions of the Durham Light Infantry gave way, gradually being forced back towards the wadi. They fought tenaciously as they withdrew through the narrow trench systems that led back to the watercourse. Supporting artillery fire was virtually non-existent, for the two sides were so close together that they intermingled. By the middle of the night, the surviving troops and tanks had been pushed right back to the edge of Wadi Zigzaou. Casualties on the British side were extremely heavy.

The corps commander, Lt. Gen. Leese, was now faced with a dilemma. He had a regiment of more powerful tanks standing by ready to attack (5th RTR with Grants and Shermans) and had a complete division of infantry (4th Indian Division) to deploy, but no secure crossing place through which to send them. Major-General Nichols was in no doubt that the lodgement had been lost and asked Leese for permission to withdraw. The decision was such a grave and critical one that Leese felt that Eighth Army's commander should be informed.

Montgomery was woken from his sleep and told by Leese that he had lost his bridgehead and requested permission to withdraw completely. Monty concurred with his corps commander and gave the word for all troops and tanks to be pulled back across the wadi and into the rear. Operation *Pugilist* was over. For the first time since Alamein, Eighth Army had met a major setback. The realization that his army was not all-conquering came as a shock to Monty and to those around him. It was a major blow to him and his prestige that an attack he had planned had failed. Even his official biographer admits that Montgomery had made a grave error in 'attempting to assault on such a narrow front over such difficult terrain'.

THE NEW ZEALAND CORPS' LEFT HOOK

By last light on 20 March, the advance guard of Lt. Gen. Freyberg's corps arrived within sight of the entrance to the Tebaga Gap. This opening between Djebel Tebaga and Djebel Melab at the extreme northern end of the Matmata Hills was just 9km wide at its narrowest point. The valley floor between the two hills had been fortified by the enemy as had the high ground overlooking the entrance. The Italian Saharan Group holding the position had perfect sight of any attempt to force a passage of the gap.

Generale Mannerini's formation consisted of around 2,500 men combined into ten companies of troops and eight batteries of artillery made up of troops from remnants of frontier guards and garrison posts in southern Libya. They were relatively untrained, not well organized and supported by a motley collection of guns of various calibres, but they did hold a commanding position which, if resolutely defended, would be a hard nut to crack.

At the sight of the arrival of the New Zealand Corps, Mannerini gave orders for all his troops to withdraw from all outposts into the main defence line. Messe had known that a large body of troops and vehicles from Eighth Army was moving through the Dahar in an attempt to outflank the Mareth positions with a diversionary attack, but had not initially realized the strength of those forces. With a whole division and an armoured brigade now heading for his back door from out of the desert, he decided that he would have to reduce his defences in the south to help stem this movement.

Orders were given for the German 164. leichte-Division to pull out of the main line and move north to strengthen the Saharan Group. The Italian Pistoia Division was to extend to its right flank to cover the gap in the Mareth defences left by the move of 164th Division. A warning order was also signalled to 21. Panzer-Division to prepare to move in support of Gen. Mannerini.

Stuart light tanks pass a knocked-out Italian armoured car in Tunisia on the drive from Gabes to Enfidaville. (DA-02009, War History Collection, Alexander Turnbull Library, Wellington NZ)

Freyberg's orders were to move against the defence line at the entrance to the Tebaga Gap in conjunction with XXX Corps' attack on the Mareth Line on the night of 20–21 March. The two operations were intended to be simultaneous and therefore problematic to Italian First Army, for Messe would then have to react to pressure from both front and rear without knowing which was the most dangerous to his positions. Freyberg complied with this by launching his first moves in the north at first light on 21 March.

The main attack started with a bombing raid by the RAF and USAAF on the defences inside the gap. Just prior to this Freyberg sent his light armour into the foothills on both sides probing the strength of enemy forces. The southern force made contact with French patrols from Force L which was screening the western side of the Matmata Hills as far as the Hallouf Pass. After the bombing raid, 8th Armoured Brigade sent its three armoured regiments and motorized infantry to probe for ways around the main defences. Most of the day was spent applying pressure but with little opportunity to break into the Italian positions. Shellfire and extensive minefields forced each move to turn back. Freyberg was not put out by the lack of progress, however, for the results of the day's activities had set the scene for a major attack.

That evening Montgomery sent a signal to Freyberg indicating that it looked as though the enemy was going to stand and fight on the main Mareth position. He therefore pressed for New Zealand Corps not just to break into the Tebaga defences, but to exploit any breakthrough into a major drive towards El Hamma and then turn southwards with mobile forces towards the Mareth Line.

During that day, the probes by 8th Armoured Brigade had determined that the heaviest defences in the gap followed the line of an old Roman wall. This in itself was not very high, but it was a metre thick and formed an anchor along which the defences were built. Just in front of the wall was a strongly defended outpost around Point 201 dominating the approaches and guarded by an extensive minefield. Lieutenant-General Freyberg realized that to get his advance moving he would have to tackle these features head on. He decided that he would launch a night attack through this minefield with infantry from Brig. Gentry's NZ 6th Brigade, capture Point 201 and then release the tanks of 8th Armoured Brigade through the gap at first light to fan out in the rear.

At 2200hrs the artillery opened up on Point 201 and the area behind. Thirty minutes later infantry from New Zealand 25th and 26th Battalions advanced in brilliant moonlight behind a rolling barrage. Sappers had opened two lanes through the minefield allowing the infantry to work their way forward uninterrupted. The advance was very successful with 6th Brigade's battalions capturing their objective by just after midnight. Casualties had been light with 11 killed and 68 wounded or missing. On the plus side the Italians lost 32 officers and 817 other ranks captured.

Brigadier Gentry was very pleased with his swift victory and suggested that 8th Armoured Brigade should not wait for first light to launch its attack, but should move through at once. Unfortunately, 8th Brigade's commander, Brig. Harvey, was less enthusiastic at attacking in the dark and decided he would stick to the original plan and go through in daylight.

When the tanks eventually tried to penetrate the gap opened up by the infantry at daylight on 22 March, the situation had changed. No longer were there just Italians facing them, but the advance elements of 21. Panzer-Division had arrived as had those of German 164. leichte-Division. The day was not one of exploitation for the tanks of 8th Armoured Brigade, but one of piecemeal attacks and withdrawals. Enemy-held high ground on both sides of the gap afforded excellent observation of events along the valley floor and the Italian gunners, quickly reinforced by their German counterparts, made life

A convoy of trucks negotiates a canal after passing through Gabes, while locals repair the crossing destroyed by the retreating Germans. (DA-03004, War History Collection, Alexander Turnbull Library, Wellington NZ)

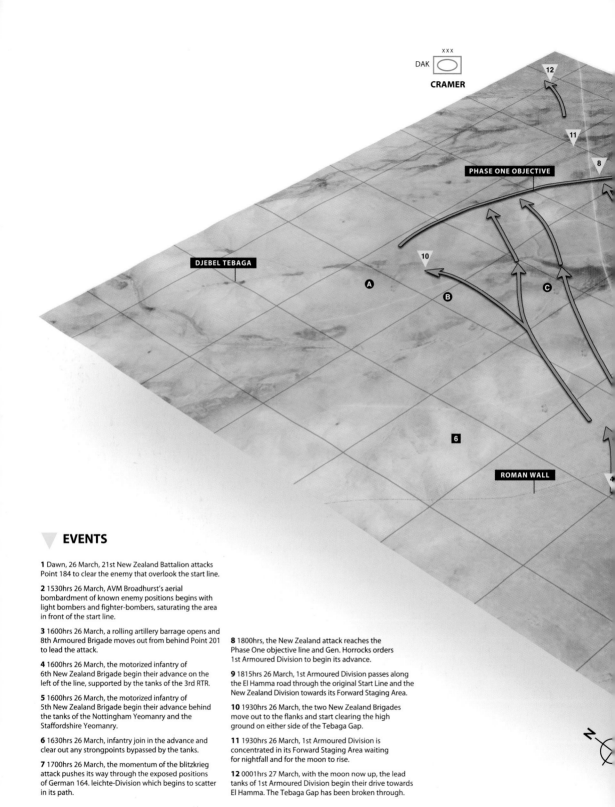

DAK ✕✕✕ ⬭ CRAMER

12

11

8

PHASE ONE OBJECTIVE

DJEBEL TEBAGA

10

A

B

C

6

ROMAN WALL

▼ EVENTS

1 Dawn, 26 March, 21st New Zealand Battalion attacks Point 184 to clear the enemy that overlook the start line.

2 1530hrs 26 March, AVM Broadhurst's aerial bombardment of known enemy positions begins with light bombers and fighter-bombers, saturating the area in front of the start line.

3 1600hrs 26 March, a rolling artillery barrage opens and 8th Armoured Brigade moves out from behind Point 201 to lead the attack.

4 1600hrs 26 March, the motorized infantry of 6th New Zealand Brigade begin their advance on the left of the line, supported by the tanks of the 3rd RTR.

5 1600hrs 26 March, the motorized infantry of 5th New Zealand Brigade begin their advance behind the tanks of the Nottingham Yeomanry and the Staffordshire Yeomanry.

6 1630hrs 26 March, infantry join in the advance and clear out any strongpoints bypassed by the tanks.

7 1700hrs 26 March, the momentum of the blitzkrieg attack pushes its way through the exposed positions of German 164. leichte-Division which begins to scatter in its path.

8 1800hrs, the New Zealand attack reaches the Phase One objective line and Gen. Horrocks orders 1st Armoured Division to begin its advance.

9 1815hrs 26 March, 1st Armoured Division passes along the El Hamma road through the original Start Line and the New Zealand Division towards its Forward Staging Area.

10 1930hrs 26 March, the two New Zealand Brigades move out to the flanks and start clearing the high ground on either side of the Tebaga Gap.

11 1930hrs 26 March, 1st Armoured Division is concentrated in its Forward Staging Area waiting for nightfall and for the moon to rise.

12 0001hrs 27 March, with the moon now up, the lead tanks of 1st Armoured Division begin their drive towards El Hamma. The Tebaga Gap has been broken through.

N

OPERATION *SUPERCHARGE II*, 26 MARCH

British X Corps attack through the Tebaga Gap in an attempt to reach El Hamma and turn the Mareth position from the rear.

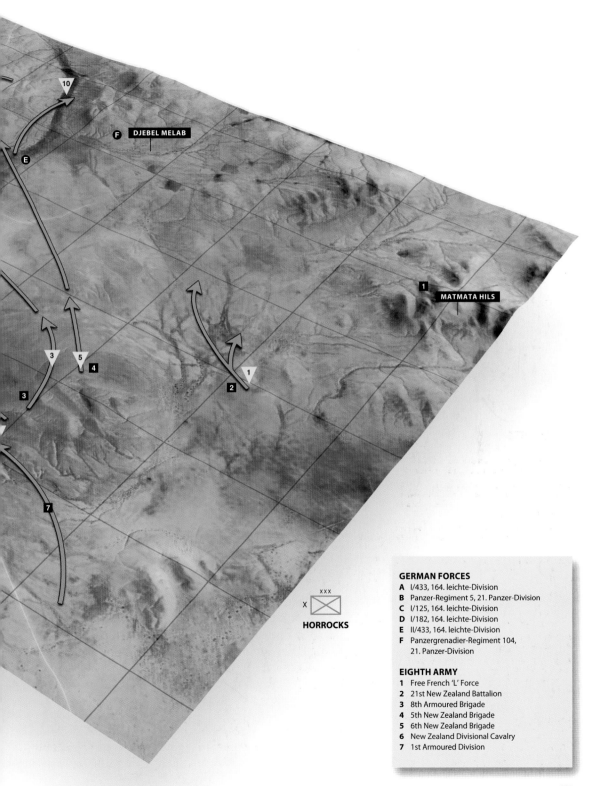

10

F **DJEBEL MELAB**

E

1

MATMATA HILS

3

5

4

1

2

3

7

X XXX

X ⊠

HORROCKS

GERMAN FORCES
A I/433, 164. leichte-Division
B Panzer-Regiment 5, 21. Panzer-Division
C I/125, 164. leichte-Division
D I/182, 164. leichte-Division
E II/433, 164. leichte-Division
F Panzergrenadier-Regiment 104,
 21. Panzer-Division

EIGHTH ARMY
1 Free French 'L' Force
2 21st New Zealand Battalion
3 8th Armoured Brigade
4 5th New Zealand Brigade
5 6th New Zealand Brigade
6 New Zealand Divisional Cavalry
7 1st Armoured Division

very difficult for the New Zealanders and the British tankers. Momentum was gradually lost that day and the next and was not to be regained for a number of days.

This failure to penetrate the Tebaga Gap was a further blow to Gen. Montgomery. The battle for the Mareth position had originally looked like it was to be a battle of two parts: a break-in and then a rapid exploitation, with an outflanking manoeuvre set to hurry things along. Unfortunately, the high optimism shown by the army commander was a little premature, for it now looked as though Gen. Messe's army was capable of containing his British opponents by the clever use of fixed defences and mobile reserves. Monty was now forced to rethink his tactics for moving his army past this roadblock.

FORCING THE TEBAGA GAP

On the morning of 23 March Montgomery settled on a new plan. He decided that he would support the flanking attack by moving 1st Armoured Division around the Matmata Hills to meet up with the New Zealanders. It would be joined by Lt. Gen. Horrocks and his X Corps' headquarters. Horrocks would then take over the running of the battle at Tebaga. The New Zealand Corps would disband and Freyberg would resort to commanding his own division. The other forces with him would come under the command of X Corps. The moves would start that night and the extra forces should be in position to launch a major assault through the Tebaga Gap towards El Hamma and Gabes on 26 March.

Montgomery was abandoning the frontal assault on the Mareth positions and trying to work around the edges. He also ordered 4th Indian Division to try a 'shorter left hook' by advancing into the Matmata Hills with two groups: one thrust would aim towards the village of Matmata itself, whilst another would go through the Hallouf Pass to the south. The first of these moves would put the Indian Division behind the main part of the Mareth Line posing an immediate threat to the rear of the Italian formations still ensconced in its fixed defences.

The route opened up by the New Zealand Corps allowed X Corps to make the move over to Tebaga in just two days. By 26 March it was ready to attack. Unfortunately, a great deal of Eighth Army's supporting artillery was not able to be brought across at such short notice with sufficient ammunition to launch a major attack. This setback proved to be something of a stimulus for further air/ground cooperation. It was suggested that Air Vice Marshal Harry Broadhurst's Desert Air Force could become an added artillery weapon.

AVM Broadhurst had been a Battle of Britain fighter pilot in 1940. Whilst a group captain he was posted to the desert as a senior staff officer and eventually advanced to command the Desert Air Force. He brought with him a lively brain and a determination to do all he could to support the ground troops of Eighth Army. The Desert Air Force had been advancing new methods of controlling its aircraft working closely with the staff at Montgomery's headquarters since before Alamein.

The question of close support for the Tebaga battle had already been receiving a lot of consideration when Montgomery's Chief of Staff, Maj. Gen. Freddie de Guingand, met with Broadhurst and asked for a 'blitz' attack to help break through the narrow gap. 'We felt that cannons from fighters might prove more deadly and disrupting to the enemy than bombs dropped from high altitude,' de Guingand later wrote. 'In view of the narrow frontage to which we were confined, this did look to be the right occasion for using the fighter in a close low-flying role over the battle area.' Broadhurst immediately agreed with the request and promised a real low-flying 'blitz', complete with bombs and cannon fire. The aircraft were to be guided by specialized ground controllers close to the front line who would be able to bring down devastating aerial bombardment on any individual target identified on the ground. It was the first time this type of control was used to vector in fighter-bombers on a large scale and led to the 'taxi rank' close support system that was so common later in the war.

Broadhurst's plan was an impressive one. The air attack was to open with a raid by three squadrons of light bombers approaching at low level to achieve surprise. As the battle progressed two and a half squadrons of Kittyhawk fighter-bombers would arrive every 15 minutes to bomb selected targets such as gun positions. At the same time, Hurricane cannon-firing tank busters would be on immediate call to break up any enemy tank concentrations. Throughout the daylight hours, Spitfire patrols of squadron strength would provide an air umbrella over the battlefield. At night, normal heavy bombing would continue attacking enemy rear areas and the next day's objectives.

The battle to force the Tebaga Gap, Operation *Supercharge II*, was planned to start at 1600hrs on 26 March, with the aerial bombardment beginning 30 minutes before. The plan was divided into two phases: Phase 1 called for the New Zealand Division to capture the enemy positions between Djebel Tebaga and Djebel Melab by advancing 4,000m beyond the Roman wall; Phase 2 would see 1st Armoured Division pass through the New Zealanders and concentrate to the north-east of their final position by last light. It would remain there until the moon came up at approximately 2315hrs when it would advance on El Hamma using the main road as its axis.

Before Operation *Supercharge II* could be launched, a preliminary move had to be made to clear the high ground around Point 184 on the slopes of Djebel Melab to deny it to the opposition. The high ground completely overlooked the start line and gave perfect observation for enemy gunners. General Freyberg sent 21st New Zealand Battalion up onto the Djebel at dawn behind a concentrated artillery barrage. By early afternoon its men had cleared enough of the Saharan Group and *Panzergrenadiers* of Panzergrenadier-Regiment 104 off the feature to allow the operation to start.

The plan was to open the attack on a two-brigade front after a barrage by the divisional artillery supported by two field and one medium regiment from X Corps. The NZ 5th Brigade would be on the right with the NZ 6th Brigade on the left. The 8th Armoured Brigade would support both attacks, advancing in front of the infantry. Once the infantry and the armoured brigades had made their breakthrough and reached the objectives of Phase 1, they were to swing to the flanks and eliminate the enemy from the high ground on both sides of the gap, leaving 1st Armoured Division to pass through.

Enemy opposition in the gap mainly consisted of German troops, all under the overall command of Gen.Lt. von Liebenstein, who also commanded 164. leichte-Division. The 21. Panzer-Division held the left flank on Djebel Melab with 164. leichte-Division on the slopes of Djebel Tebaga; the dividing line between them was the road passing through the gap towards El Hamma. Mixed in with these formations were units from Gen. Mannerini's Saharan Group. The 15. Panzer-Division was still to the

THE 4TH INDIAN DIVISION APPLIES PRESSURE TO THE MARETH LINE DEFENCES BY LAUNCHING AN OUTFLANKING ATTACK THROUGH THE MATMATA HILLS (pp. 80–81)

Sikh soldiers of 4th Indian Division launch an infantry attack through the low mountains that flanked the Mareth defences **(1)**. The division was attempting a shorter left hook to get behind the Axis main line whilst the New Zealanders engineered a much wider sweep to outflank the whole of the Axis positions. Opposing the division in the hills were various isolated Italian units strengthened by elements from the German 164. leichte-Division.

The 4th Indian Division had been in action in North Africa since its formation in 1939 and had an impressive reputation for its fighting ability. It took part in many actions in the region including the East African campaign of 1940 and Syria in 1941. It was part of Wavell's forces in the early North African battles and held the Ruweisat Ridge during both actions at El Alamein. After the second battle it was dispersed only to be re-formed just before the events at Mareth.

The division consisted of battalions of infantry from many of the leading Indian regiments with its men coming from a variety of religious and ethnic backgrounds including contingents from

the Muslim, Hindu and Sikh faiths. The division was usually composed of two Indian brigades (taken from 5th, 7th and 11th Indian Brigades) and one British.

Soldiers who followed the Sikh faith were allowed to wear their pagri headdress (the turban) in action **(2)**. Their religion required them to grow their hair long and to cover it with the pagri. Attempts were made to make these men wear the standard steel helmet in battle, but their religious convictions required them to decline to do so. Events later showed that Sikhs suffered no more head injuries than any other section of the military. It was widely believed that a Sikh turban could stop a bullet. Lieutenant-General Sir Reginald Savory later explained: 'The turban is, in itself, a very effective buffer. I have known Sikhs pick bullets out of their turbans during and after battle. The turban absorbs the shock of a bullet possibly rather better than a tin helmet.' Although such a view was most likely apocryphal, the turban was, none the less, proven protection against the various knocks and blows to the head that are commonly suffered in action.

The picture was originally captioned as being of the 'Gabes Gap' which could mean the road leading to the Tebaga Gap or between El Hamma and Gabes. It might even be the road through the Wadi Akarit lines. Wherever it is, it gives a good impression of the terrain that was fought through and demonstrates the amount of work required by sappers to keep it open. (IWM, NA1811)

south-east. It had withdrawn from the front of the Mareth Line into a position that shadowed the New Zealand Division's activities, but was not committed to the defence of the gap. The 10. Panzer-Division was still north of Gabes countering the movement of US II Corps which had taken Maknassy and was pushing towards Gafsa threatening to break through to the coast. Intelligence suggested that 21. Panzer-Division had 44 tanks available and 15. Panzer-Division just 29.

Despite the success in blunting Montgomery's attack on the Mareth Line, Arnim could see that the pressure being applied at Tebaga and around Maknassy would eventually lead to a breakthrough. He was worried that Messe's army might well be cut off completely. On 24 March he gave the order for the Mareth Line to be gradually given up. Both Kesselring and Messe were against this and urged the army group commander to consider a counterattack instead, but Arnim would not be moved. He insisted that the withdrawal should begin on 25 March and was to be completed within three days. The Italian divisions in the line were to pull back to the Wadi Akarit position where they would make another stand against the inexorable progress of Eighth Army.

Operation *Supercharge II* began immediately after preliminary aerial and artillery bombardments at 1600hrs on 26 March. First to move out were the tanks of 8th Armoured Brigade, rolling forwards from their forming-up point behind the shelter of Point 201. They moved cautiously forwards behind a creeping barrage with the direction of their front line marked by coloured smoke. Each regiment advanced with its heavier Grant and Sherman tanks in the lead. Behind this shield, New Zealand infantry, transported in carriers, followed on. Then came the second line of armour, lighter Crusader tanks, with their own carriers tucked in behind. Finally, when all of this mobile force had passed through the enemy minefields, mortar and artillery fire and breached the Roman wall, the leading foot soldiers joined in the attack.

Machine-gun nests that were bypassed by the tanks were eliminated by the infantry. Unmarked minefields caused some casualties to both men and armour and rocky ground sometimes made the going difficult, but the sheer weight of the attack kept the momentum going at a steady pace. Overhead, Broadhurst's fighter-bombers arrived in relays of 30 aircraft every 15 minutes, swooping down on any identified opposition that had been vectored in by the forward controllers housed in tanks close to the start line. They blasted machine-gun posts, artillery positions and any concentrations of German tanks that tried to oppose the ground attack. British tanks and New Zealand infantry rolled relentlessly over the enemy and swept their way forwards with fire and shot in just the kind of blitzkrieg attack that had been foreseen in the planning stages. In the attack, 8th Armoured Brigade lost 12 Shermans, one Grant and three Crusaders.

For the next two hours the massive attack pressed on relentlessly, then, right on cue at around 1800hrs, the New Zealanders reached their main objective and signalled for Phase 2 of Operation *Supercharge II* to begin. The leading regiments from 2nd Armoured Brigade of 1st Armoured Division now motored forward at 1800hrs as planned, with Brigadier Fisher instructing his tanks to 'speed up, straight through, no halting'. By 1930hrs the division was on its first staging halt. Here it laagered in a concentration area some six kilometres in front of the New Zealanders, gathering strength and waiting for night to fall and the moon to rise. At 2300hrs, just as the moon did appear, preparations were made to continue the advance. At 0001hrs on 27 March the lead tanks moved out heading straight for El Hamma.

Generalleutnant von Liebenstein had watched the attack unfold during the early evening with increasing trepidation. The strength and direction of the attack was carving its way through his best units; the two centre battalions of 164. leichte-Division were overrun and 21. Panzer had its Panzer-Regiment 5 pushed aside with the loss of 12 tanks and a battalion of Panzergrenadier-Regiment 125 scattered. El Hamma and the road to Gabes would soon be open to an armoured thrust by the British which would seal the fate of those forces holding the Mareth positions. Liebenstein ordered units of 21. Panzer-Division to fall back to a position 6km in front of El Hamma and place an anti-tank screen across its approaches. He also requested 15. Panzer-Division to attack the enemy on his left flank.

During the night the British armoured advance gathered pace driving down the road towards El Hamma, ploughing through exposed German positions and scattering Panzergrenadiers before it. Liebenstein now ordered all units on his left to disengage and fall back to a position south-west of El Hamma.

The retreat became a race with the British to see who could move fastest, with both sides moving parallel to each other and often becoming mixed together in the confusion. The Germans won the race and managed to get enough force in place to man an anti-tank screen across the approaches to El Hamma which stopped 1st Armoured Division in its tracks. Trouble erupted in the British rear when 15. Panzer-Division attacked from the south-east trying to get at the division's flanks. This effort by the German tanks was beaten off by the efficient use of heavy 17-pdr anti-tank guns and the Sherman tanks of 8th Armoured Brigade.

Dawn found the lead tanks of 2nd Armoured Brigade stalled in front of the German anti-tank screen and hemmed in by high ground on both sides. The 15. Panzer-Division, still with about 50 fit tanks, moved north-west to join with 21. Panzer-Division and then struck at the eastern flank of the British armour. Throughout the day constant opposition by the German Panzers frustrated every attempt to reach El Hamma. Operation *Supercharge II* was gradually running out of steam.

Lieutenant-General Horrocks ordered the division to stand fast whilst the New Zealand Division came up to join them prior to launching another set-piece infantry/armour attack. Unfortunately, Freyberg's division was still fighting with remnants of German 164. leichte-Division in the high ground on either side of the gap and required some time before it could reorganize and move to the north-west. Eventually, at 1630hrs that day, the New Zealanders were ordered to move up to join 1st Armoured Division during the night. Freyberg was then asked by Horrocks if he could mount another *Supercharge II* type of attack to break through to El Hamma.

Lieutenant-General Freyberg was unhappy with Horrocks' suggestion, indicating that he would rather bypass El Hamma and move directly on Gabes. Horrocks was not sure about this, for Montgomery had ordered that the advance should use the roads through El Hamma to keep the lines of communication open. The matter was referred to Eighth Army's commander and more time was lost. In the event, circumstances made a final decision rather academic, for during the 27th Messe had speeded up his withdrawal from the Mareth Line and almost all of his force had escaped northwards through Gabes. The respite also allowed the two Panzer divisions to regroup ready for their own withdrawal.

When the general giving up of the Mareth Line was finally recognized by Eighth Army, XXX Corps was ordered to follow up immediately. This coincided

Troops from 4th Indian Division watch from a lorry as a squadron of Valentine tanks passes them somewhere along a road across the flat coastal plain. The divisional sign of a red eagle can be seen above the 92 on the back of the truck. (IWM, NA1994)

with 4th Indian Division's completion of its trek through the Matmata Hills to reach a point behind the Axis defences as part of Montgomery's 'short left hook' only to find that the enemy had flown. There was little fighting in the south on 28 March as the last of Messe's mobile forces fled northwards, whilst in the north the two Panzer divisions stubbornly refused to withdraw from around El Hamma. When, on the night of 28–29 March, word came from Messe that all of the units to the south had been withdrawn, Liebenstein finally received the order to pull his tanks back behind the line at Wadi Akarit.

The end of the battle of the Mareth Line was something of an anticlimax. The New Zealand Division and 1st Armoured Brigade were ordered on 28 March to close up on the line El Hamma–Gabes where the Panzers were holding out, but not to engage the enemy in a major attack. Leese's XXX Corps was to pass through and advance until contact was made with the enemy. All strength was to be conserved for the next likely operation which was to attack the new enemy positions at Wadi Akarit

The battle of Mareth had been won, but its winning had not been convincing. It took much longer to complete than was planned and was achieved by force of numbers rather than by tactical brilliance. If the main attack had been strong and forced its way into the enemy defences, Messe's armour would have been committed in the south which would have allowed Freyberg's New Zealanders to exploit their left hook in the north. By attacking fixed defences with just one brigade when so much infantry and armour was available to him, Montgomery had made a severe miscalculation. In contrast, his switching of his main effort to what was intended to be a flanking manoeuvre was a bold move and one which eventually brought victory. However, the delay in organizing this effort allowed Messe sufficient time to switch his forces to oppose it. When it became clear that the position at Mareth had been lost, this respite allowed Messe to pull all of his forces out of the line and withdraw them to a new position relatively unmolested. The escape of these troops to fight another day made the victory rather a hollow one. Cracks were beginning to show in the Eighth Army commander's invincibility.

THE END IN AFRICA

Eighth Army was unable to exploit the breakthrough because of Liebenstein's determination to shield the withdrawal from the Mareth positions. It was not until 29 March that the enemy relinquished its hold on the El Hamma–Gabes line and withdrew at speed to the north to get behind the hastily prepared positions at Wadi Akarit some 20km beyond Gabes. Fighter-bombers of the Desert Air Force harassed them all the way.

The Italians had been busy digging and strengthening a line which stretched along a 'pinch point' on the coastal plain between the sea and the impenetrable salt flats of the Chott El Fedjadj. This position was much shorter than at Mareth, just 24km wide across the flat open countryside bordering the sea and up into a semicircle of steep-sided hills which overlooked the Wadi Akarit. The hills had several gaps through which troops could pass once they had traversed the defended coastal plain. The wadi was wider and deeper than the Wadi Zigzaou at Mareth near the sea, but as it rose up towards the hills it flattened out into no more than a dip. The Italians had had time to dig a new anti-tank ditch in front of the western end of the wadi and to excavate trenches and sow minefields along the most vulnerable parts of the line, including the gaps through the hills.

German prisoners from 15. Panzer-Division in a POW compound at Gafsa. They were captured in the fighting between El Hamma and Gabes. (IWM, NA1804)

The Eighth Army advance after the battle for the Mareth Line

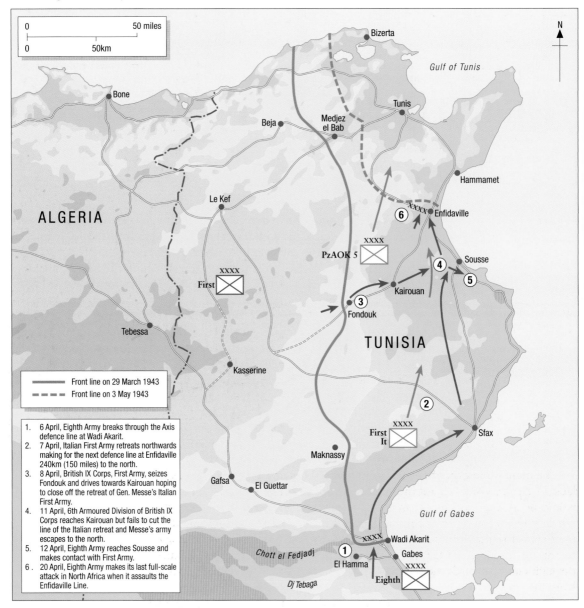

Scale:
- 0 — 50 miles
- 0 — 50km

N

Key places and labels on map: Bizerta, Gulf of Tunis, Bone, Tunis, Beja, Medjez el Bab, Hammamet, Le Kef, ALGERIA, Enfidaville, PzAOK 5, Sousse, First, Kairouan, Fondouk, Tebessa, TUNISIA, Kasserine, Maknassy, First It, Sfax, Gafsa, El Guettar, Gulf of Gabes, Chott el Fedjadj, Wadi Akarit, El Hamma, Gabes, Dj Tebaga, Eighth

Front line on 29 March 1943
Front line on 3 May 1943

1. 6 April, Eighth Army breaks through the Axis defence line at Wadi Akarit.
2. 7 April, Italian First Army retreats northwards making for the next defence line at Enfidaville 240km (150 miles) to the north.
3. 8 April, British IX Corps, First Army, seizes Fondouk and drives towards Kairouan hoping to close off the retreat of Gen. Messe's Italian First Army.
4. 11 April, 6th Armoured Division of British IX Corps reaches Kairouan but fails to cut the line of the Italian retreat and Messe's army escapes to the north.
5. 12 April, Eighth Army reaches Sousse and makes contact with First Army.
6 . 20 April, Eighth Army makes its last full-scale attack in North Africa when it assaults the Enfidaville Line.

The defences were manned in the most part by Italian formations. From west to east they consisted of the Saharan Group and German 164. leichte-Division in the hills on the right of the line; then the Italian 'Pistoia', 'Spezia' and 'Trieste' Divisions in the centre of the plain and then, finally, part of German 90. leichte-Division and the Italian Young Fascist Division in the sector nearest the sea which carried the main coastal highway. Support to the defences was provided by the 88mm guns of the Luftwaffe's 19. Flak-Division. The 15. Panzer-Division along with the remainder of 90. leichte-Division were in the rear ready to counterattack any breakthrough. The 10. and 21. Panzer-Divisionen together with the Italian 'Centauro' division was to the north-west screening the Americans near El Guettar.

The end in Africa

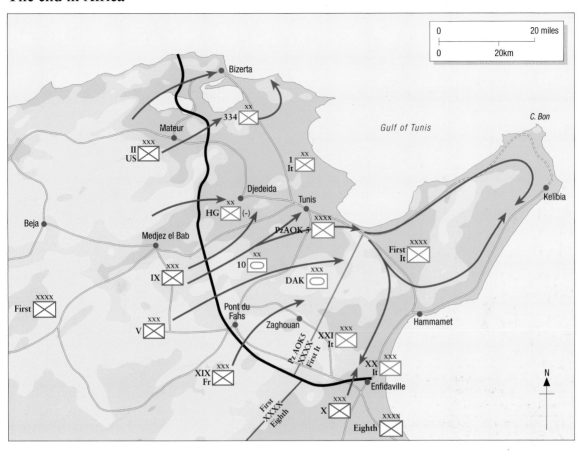

The main limitation of the Wadi Akarit position as a defence line was its lack of depth. Once across the wadi and through the hills, Eighth Army would be able to spread out on the gradually widening coastal plain to the north where its superiority in numbers and motorized formations could be put to effective use. Another major drawback was the presence of US II Corps to the north-west. If Lt. Gen. Patton's corps could continue its advance through Gafsa towards the coast, it could outflank the Wadi Akarit position from the rear.

On 30 March, Lt. Gen. Horrocks' X Corps, following up the enemy retreat, soon brushed up against the defences at Wadi Akarit. It was suggested that if Montgomery would accept heavy casualties there was a possibility that an immediate blitzkrieg attack would carry Eighth Army straight through the enemy line. The proposition was put to Montgomery, but he declined to make such a bold move, deciding to go for his usual set-piece attack strategy which he followed for the remainder of the war. In the meantime there was, he reasoned, a prospect of the enemy withdrawing once again if faced with an overwhelming show of strength. If both Eighth Army and US II Corps acted in concert, then the Axis command might decide that the position was untenable. In fact this was just what they were thinking for, on 29 February, Ambrosio in Rome indicated to Arnim that he must hold the southern flank stubbornly, but if AOK 1 was in immediate danger of destruction, it was to withdraw to a new position at Enfidaville.

Generale Messe presents himself to Gen. Montgomery after capture in Tunisia. It was towards the end of the campaign that Monty found out he had not been fighting Rommel for the last two months, much to his disappointment. He had been hoping to take the surrender of the German field marshal. (IWM, NA2886)

The plan for the assault on the Wadi Akarit position called for XXX Corps to make the attack and for X Corps to pass through with upwards of 500 tanks once the line had been broken, although 7th Armoured Division was to be kept in reserve. It would open with three infantry divisions. The Indian 4th Division and British 50th and 51st Divisions would attack the centre of the enemy positions held by the 'Spezia' and 'Trieste' Divisions. A feint move by 1st Armoured Division of X Corps would be made simultaneously on the hills on the western edge of the enemy defences.

The operation began at 0500hrs on 6 April. Eighth Army had spent the previous week regrouping ready for the assault whilst the enemy was pounded almost continually by British and American air forces. After a heavy softening-up artillery barrage, 51st Division advanced on the right, 50th Division in the centre and the Indian 4th Division on the left. Most resistance came in the centre where an anti-tank ditch and the deep wadi held up 50th Division. Fighting was fierce in the steep hills beyond the wadi, but the overwhelming numbers of infantry ground down the opposition. By mid-morning Messe could see that the main danger was in the middle of the line and began moving 164. leichte-Division across from its position in the western hills. In the afternoon he committed the 15. Panzer-Division when 8th Armoured Brigade and the New Zealanders of British X Corps penetrated the positions held by the 'Trieste' Division which had been opened up by 51st Division. The 10. and 21. Panzer-Divisionen were also ordered to switch from facing Gen. Patton's US II Corps and move towards the British attack. This should have been the cue for Patton to drive through and meet up with Eighth Army and take the whole of the Wadi Akarit battlefield from the rear, but the Americans were apparently in no position to make such a bold move.

By the end of the afternoon Messe knew that his army would be unable to hold the line for another day. The British were forming bridgeheads in many places and ammunition was almost all gone. At 1700hrs he reported the dire situation to Arnim. Kesselring and the Italian command in Rome urged the army group commander to continue resisting, but Arnim replied that the situation was hopeless and he was pulling AOK 1 back to the Enfidaville position some 240km to the north. At 2000hrs he gave the order to Messe for mobile units to begin the retreat; those troops without transport should start walking.

Eighth Army began the pursuit of the enemy at 1000hrs the next day, overhauling stragglers and fighting small rearguards on the way. The collapse of Messe's army at Wadi Akarit marked the beginning of the end in Africa. The strong natural defences of the position were unable to withstand the great force applied with unremitting pressure by Eighth Army. Over 7,000 Axis troops were captured after the battle, most of them Italians who could see no point in continuing the struggle. Those that escaped the debacle were in a sorry state. Eighth Army had 1,289 casualties in the attack and had lost 32 tanks.

More problems arose for Arnim when Lt. Gen. Anderson's First Army stepped up its pressure from the west. As Messe retreated northwards and Eighth Army followed up, there was no longer any need for US II Corps to attack from Gafsa towards the sea. The American formation was then shifted to the north coast of Tunisia to conduct operations there. The decision was not met with enthusiasm by the Americans. They felt that after much heavy fighting against crack German forces, they were being shunted to the north of Tunisia to make way for the all-conquering British Eighth Army. This was partially true, for neither Montgomery nor 18th Army Group Commander, Gen. Alexander, was impressed by the performance of II Corps and its slow progress east of Gafsa and preferred to stick with Eighth Army for the advance to Tunis.

With Messe's army withdrawing northwards towards Enfidaville, there was a good opportunity for Anderson's forces to strike eastwards to intercept it. On 4 April, before the start of the Wadi Akarit battle, IX Corps was ordered to seize positions near Kairouan which would enable its 6th Armoured Division to attack the roads over which AOK 1 would have to pass. The division would, depending on what time it reached the area, either block the way or hit the

A picture that sums up the futility of the last few months of the fighting; acres and acres of Axis prisoners. After Alamein, Rommel had always thought that the campaign in North Africa was a lost cause. The numbers of the enemy captured in Tunisia were greater than those lost by the Germans at Stalingrad. (IWM, NA2864)

Axis retreat in the flank. As it turned out, IX Corps failed to deliver and Messe retreated past Kairouan unmolested.

Arnim's army group was now being pushed back in every sector. Much fighting was still to be done before it could finally be surrounded and captured. Even though the end was inevitable, the Axis powers in Rome and Berlin ordered it to fight on. On the very day that the line at Wadi Akarit broke, Hitler and Mussolini met in Salzburg and agreed that Tunisia must be held, whatever the cost, to keep Allied forces engaged in North Africa rather than allow them to invade Europe.

All the main formations of AOK 1 were back in the Enfidaville area by 12 April. On the same day the British captured Sousse 40km to the south and made contact with IX Corps of First Army near Kairouan to join up the whole of the Allied front in Southern Tunisia. The next day they made contact with the outposts of the Enfidaville positions.

The scene was now set for both Allied armies to make the drive on Tunis and finish off Axis forces in North Africa. The campaign in Tunisia had reached its terminal stage. In the final month of the fighting, First Army put four corps into the drive to reach Tunis. From north to south US II Corps, British V Corps, British IX Corps and the French XIX Corps attacked in unison, pushing back the front line across mountain, valley and plain against an enemy able to resist fiercely, but unable to hold ground. Each of these corps suffered large numbers of casualties, often with little immediate progress, in the attempt to finish off the campaign and reach Tunis. On the eastern part of the front along the coast Eighth Army struck at the enemy positions around Enfidaville with X Corps. The 4th Indian Division and the New Zealand Division cleared the two peaks of high ground, Djebel Garci and Takrouna, which overlooked the area north of Enfidaville town whilst the newly arrived 56th Division gained battlefield experience probing the enemy defences to the north.

The resistance met on the Enfidaville Line caused a rethink by both the army group commander, Gen. Alexander, and Montgomery. Plugging away at the coastal route would involve high casualties to Eighth Army at a time when it was being considered for the forthcoming invasion of Sicily. Alexander decided that Eighth Army would continue with local operations, but would hold back on a full-blown assault of the line. The main thrust to bring down the Axis regime was now to be made by First Army and Alexander ordered Montgomery to give up some of his formations to reinforce Anderson's operations. Montgomery transferred 7th Armoured Division, 4th Indian Division and 201st Guards Brigade from Eighth Army to First Army.

Thus reinforced, First Army launched its final offensive Operation *Strike* on 3 May. Tunis fell on the 7th and six days later it was all over. Commander of Heeresgruppe Afrika, Gen. von Arnim, surrendered his forces on 13 May and between 250,000 and 300,000 Axis troops marched into captivity. The North African Campaign was over.

THE BATTLEFIELD TODAY

At the time of writing, the revolutions enacted during the 'Arab Spring' have changed the shape of North Africa. The countries through which Eighth Army fought, Egypt, Libya and Tunisia, are about to become fledgling democracies. Whether these changes are for the better will remain to be seen. It may take some years before the security of the individual can be guaranteed, but when it is, the region will become a fascinating area for the battlefield visitor. Before then, if visiting these countries to see the scenes of the action, it might be prudent to book with a reputable battlefield tour operator who knows the situation and the area well.

Before all the upheavals, Tunisia had a thriving tourist trade. Visitors mainly flocked to the beaches and holiday resorts in the north. Nonetheless, more intrepid explorers could venture into the area of the Mareth Line to see the remains of the defences and to visit the small museum dedicated to the battle. Unlike any other battlefield in North Africa, there are concrete remains of a fixed defensive line to explore. So many other scenes of the conflict elsewhere remain barren featureless spots where it is difficult to pinpoint the action. The Mareth Line is a welcome exception to this.

FURTHER READING AND BIBLIOGRAPHY

One of the most important books covering Rommel's retreat and the battle of Mareth is the *British Official History of the Mediterranean and Middle East Volume IV*. This gives the main view of the factual details of the offensive and its outcome. *The Rommel Papers* is always a good start to find out the intimate thoughts of the German commander, and George Forty's *The Armies of Rommel* fills in many details regarding the Axis forces. Good contemporary accounts of the advance from Alamein to Mareth and the battle itself exist in the National Archives at Kew, the most interesting of which can be found in the WO201 and WO204 series.

Anon, *The Tiger Kills*, HMSO: London, 1944

Braddock, D. W., *The Campaigns in Egypt and Libya 1940–1942*, Gale and Polden: Aldershot, 1964

Carver, Michael, *Dilemmas of the Desert War: The Libyan Campaign 1940–1942*, Batsford: London, 1986

de Guingand, Maj. Gen. Sir Francis, *Operation Victory*, Hodder & Stoughton: London, 1947

Delaney, John, *Fighting the Desert Fox*, Arms and Armour: London, 1998

Forty, George, *The Armies of Rommel*, Arms and Armour: London, 1997

Fraser, David, *Knight's Cross: The Life of Field Marshal Erwin Rommel*, Harper Collins: London, 1993

Hamilton, Nigel, *Monty: Master of the Battlefield 1942–1944*, Hamish Hamilton: London, 1983

Irving, David, *The Trail of the Fox: The Life of Field Marshal Irwin Rommel*, Weidenfeld & Nicholson: London, 1977

Joslen, Lt. Col. H. F., *Orders of Battle: Second World War 1939–1945*, HMSO: London, 1960

Liddell Hart, Capt. B. H. (ed), *The Rommel Papers*, Collins: London, 1953

——, *The Tanks: The History of the Royal Tank Regiment, Volume Two*, Cassell: London, 1959

Playfair, Maj. Gen. S. O., *The Mediterranean and Middle East, Volume IV*, HMSO: London, 1966

Verney, Maj. Gen. G. L., *The Desert Rats: The History of the 7th Armoured Division*, Hutchinson: London, 1954

INDEX